BATTERED *to* BLESSED
My Personal Journey

ALSO BY BRENDA WALSH,
WITH LINDA JOHNSON AND CINDA SANNER

Cooking With the Micheff Sisters

ALSO BY KAY RIZZO

A Place in God's Heart

Elizabeth, An Adventist Girl (four-volume set)

I Will Die Free

For His Honor

Charlie Jones

BATTERED *to* BLESSED
My Personal Journey

BRENDA WALSH
with Kay D. Rizzo

3ABN BOOKS

P.O. Box 220 West Frankfort, Illinois
www.3ABN.org

Pacific Press® Publishing Association
Nampa, Idaho
Oshawa, Ontario, Canada
www.pacificpress.com

Edited by Kay Kuzma
Book and cover design © by Mark Bond for BON Design, Inc.
Cover photo © Brenda McClearen

Library of Congress Cataloging-in-Publication Data

Walsh, Brenda, 1953-
Battered to blessed : my personal story / Brenda Walsh and Kay D. Rizzo.
p.cm.
ISBN 13: 978-0-8163-2067-7
ISBN 10: 0-8163-2067-5
1. Walsh, Brenda, 1953- 2. Seventh-day Adventists—United States—Biography.
3. Christian biography—United States. 4. Wife abuse—United States.
5. Television in religion—United States. I. Rizzo, Kay D., 1943- II. Title.

BX6193.W24 2005
286.7'092—dc22
[B]   2004065475

Additional copies of this book are available from two locations:
3ABN: Call 1-800-752-3226 or visit http://www.3abn.org
Adventist Book Centers: Call 1-800-765-6955
or visit http://www.adventistbookcenter.com

08 09 10 · 5 4 3

—Dedication—

I want to dedicate this book first and foremost to my Lord and Savior, Jesus Christ. I tremble to think where I would be right now without You. You heard my cry and brought me out of a horrible pit, out of the miry clay, and set my feet upon a rock, and established my steps. You put a new song in my mouth. Praise to my God! Because of what You have done for me, many will see that You can do the same for them. You are my awesome God! I love You, Jesus!

I also want to dedicate this book to my husband, Tim. You have stood faithfully by my side and supported me in whatever God has asked me to do. Your willing and giving heart has touched my life in a very special way. I want to thank you for always wanting the best for me, for encouraging me to go on even when everything looked impossible, and for being not only my husband but my most trusted friend. For your listening ear and wise advice but most of all for your unconditional love I love you, honey!

—Brenda

—ACKNOWLEDGMENTS—

My heartfelt thanks to so many people without whom this book would not have been possible:

To my precious parents—thank you for all the love and support you have always given me. Thank you for not judging me but loving me through the pain. But most of all, thank you for introducing me to Jesus. Mom and Dad, I share your dream that "someday all our family will be together in heaven, with not one lost." I love you both with all my heart!

To my sisters, Linda and Cinda—you are my best friends. I can't imagine my life without you in it. I thank you for your laughter, patience, advice, honesty, and most of all, your love. *Kids Time* would not be the same without your loving support. What a privilege it is to work with you in God's ministry. I love you very much!

To my brothers, Jim and Ken—no words can describe how special you are to me and how very proud I am of you both. I thank God for each of you. I admire you for your willingness to always put God and family first. Thank you for all the sacrifices you made for me. I love you dearly.

To my girls, Becky and Linda Kay—you are the light of my life! The joy you have brought to my life is immeasurable. I thank God for the privilege of watching you grow, and I am so proud of the women you have become. You are so precious to me. I love you both with all my heart.

To my grandson, Michael—you will always be "Grandma's boy," for you have completely stolen my heart. You are the sunshine of my life.

To my treasured friends, Marie, Carole, Susan, Bonnie, Rita, Jan, Peg, Nancy, Sally, Mecca, Margie, and Mildred—I'm deeply grateful for the fun times we've shared, the times you've lifted me up, and all the precious memories. You will always have my love.

To Three Angels Broadcasting Network—thank you for the privilege of serving Jesus through this worldwide ministry; and to you, Danny, for inspiring me to do more for Jesus.

To Bobby Davis—I so appreciate your support, and the encouragement to capture on tape "My Cookie Story," thus making it possible for others to receive a blessing too.

To Kay Kuzma for your advice, wisdom, and endless hours editing this book. You have my deepest respect and admiration. You are my mentor and treasured friend.

To Shelley Quinn and Mollie Steenson for your honesty, friendship, and shoulder to lean on, but most of all for your Christian love. We will be neighbors in heaven!

And last but not least, to Kay Rizzo, an incredibly gifted author, for being willing to take my words and make them come to life. For this I am deeply grateful.

—Brenda

—Contents—

—INTRODUCTION—

The breakfast dishes are done and put away, and I head upstairs to my office to start answering the latest mound of letters that I have received as the producer and host of the *Kids Time* television program for Three Angels Broadcasting Network (3ABN). As I open one letter and then another, I can't help stopping to say a prayer of thanks for so many blessings. The letters all begin the same: *"Dear Miss Brenda . . ."*

One in particular catches my attention. It's from a girl in London, England:

Dear Miss Brenda,

I just want to write and thank you for Kids Time. I just love it and I watch it every day. My mum says that since I've started watching Kids Time that I have been minding her more and that she has seen a change in me. I'm eleven years old and I try and share Jesus with someone every day just like you said we should do. Today I sat with a girl at school that nobody likes. I tried to be nice to her and even played with her at break time. I think I shared Jesus, what do you think?

Can you please sign me up for Kids Club? I want to learn more about Jesus. My mum says that maybe we can go to church sometime. My dad doesn't live with us anymore. It makes me really sad. Can you please pray for my dad so he will love my mum again?

I love you, Miss Brenda, I want to grow up to be just like you.

Love, Tara

I stop and say a prayer for Tara and her mom and dad before I continue. My heart is touched as I read the next letter. This one is from a father in Iraq:

Dear Miss Brenda,

The warmest greetings to you and all the children everywhere in the world that your wonderful program reaches. I am writing to you with much thankfulness for your program, Kids Time. My children are young and my wife would like to know more about your God to teach our children. Please, Miss Brenda, can she obtain your studies from Kids Club or is she too old? We are very willing to pay for these important studies. We want our children to grow up to do good deeds that you speak of. We want them to know your Jesus. Even I as a father am learning very much from your program. I want my children to be good children.

Sincerely, Isam

Again, I am overwhelmed with how blessed I am and with the realization of how far-reaching this ministry is. God is using *Kids Time* to reach children—and adults—all over the world, and I count it a great privilege to be used by God in such a special way. It is an awesome responsibility, and I don't take it lightly. I open the next letter, pausing to look at the return address. It is from Kisumu, Kenya. It reads:

Dear Miss Brenda,

Receive my greetings in the mighty name of Jesus Christ. How are you? I am fine in Christ my Savior. My name is Penina, and I am seventeen years old. I like singing, and reading the Bible, and watching programs. I especially like the programs which touch me spiritually, like your Kids Time program.

Miss Brenda, I'm really appreciating your work and I would like to encourage you to continue with it for God has very good plans for you. Sincerely speaking, Miss Brenda, I've gained a lot from your program, and I know I will gain more as I continue watching it. I love Kids Time very much and I get excited when seeing the children sing.

My main reason for writing is that I'm kindly requesting you to allow me to join the Kids Club. I will be very happy if you will allow me to be a member, as I know I will enjoy the lessons.

Miss Brenda, although we are physically separated, please let us spiritually remain together. Remember, I have seen you but you have not seen me. I will send you a photo of myself so you can see what I look like. Please know that I always smile with you, sing with you, and I love you Miss Brenda very much.

May God bless you,
Yours faithfully, Penina

Brenda at the studio controls at 3ABN.

After reading the letter again, I return it to its envelope to read later on the air. I can feel the tears welling up in my eyes. I am overcome with emotion as I think of these children and young people who look up to "Miss Brenda."

Why me, Lord? I am not worthy. My mind cannot help drifting through my past, and I shudder to think of all the mistakes I made along the way—mistakes that cost me dearly, and all because I did not lean on Jesus!

I have struggled with how I could help others avoid these mistakes. At the same time, I feel compelled to share how great God is, for no matter how deep you get yourself into trouble, He can pull you out! He has plans for your life, plans for good and not for evil. I'm a living testimony that with God nothing is impossible, and that is why I have written this book. Yes, there are some "dark" scenes described, but I want everyone to understand just how evil sin really is, in contrast to just how good God is!

I made some pretty foolish mistakes. That is what always happens when you don't make Jesus first and foremost in your life. I took prescription drugs that I had no business taking. I fell into a relationship in which I was abused, beaten, and left for dead. I thought my life was over. But God took the ashes of my life and made me whole again. He gave me a loving family and the most challenging job I could ever imagine, producing children's programming for an international television network!

As you read this book, notice that each step of the way I have always loved Jesus, but I had not totally surrendered my life to Him. Even though I prayed to God, I was depending on myself to fix my problems. I let pride get in the way.

I learned through painful lessons that there is no better place to be than living the life that God has planned for us. If we depend on self, we will always fail. There is no safer place to be than in the arms of Jesus. And there is no greater joy than serving Jesus!

Above all else, I want to encourage you to give your heart to Jesus and totally surrender your will to Him. If you are hurting or your life seems worthless and empty, ask Jesus to come into your life and just watch the miracles that begin to happen!

I don't tell my story to bring Satan any glory but only to lift up Jesus as Lord and Savior. It is my prayer that when you finish reading this book you will totally surrender your life to God and desire a closer walk with Him. Jesus worked a miracle in my life. He redeemed me, and He will do the same for you.

If Only . . .

Where does a story truly begin? In life there are few clear-cut moments when we can look back and say, "Everything started here." Yet, there are those times when a one-minute decision can trigger a sequence of unforeseen events that set disastrous and irrevocable consequences into motion.

All is quiet in the house. I stare at my blank computer screen. The blinking cursor scolds me for not writing something, anything. It's two o'clock in the morning. My husband is asleep upstairs. I wish I could join him. I have to work tomorrow morning. But alas, I'm wide awake.

It's not because I'm uncertain of my story. I know that all too well. I've lived with the agonizing memories for thirty-one years. The events are seared into my mind. I'm discovering that dragging so much pain from the deepest recesses of my consciousness and putting it on paper is proving to be more difficult than I could ever have imagined.

I've never told anyone outside my family the details of what happened to me. It would be so much easier to forget about it, to let it go, to move on. But I can't. Many don't realize just how terrible sin really is. Satan's goal is to bring us pain, heartache, guilt, and shame. Jesus died to give us life—and to give it to us more abundantly!

The time has come to speak out. I am convinced that I must tell my story, not to parade my past before a curious crowd but to glorify and honor my Father's holy name. For if He can bring beauty out of the ashes of my life, you can be assured that He will do the same for you.

CHAPTER 1

Little Decisions, Big Consequences

How fragile a life can be so easily broken, so hard to mend.
—Unknown

I was in love with life.

I had grown up in a very conservative and loving home. I loved the Lord but had never really given Him first place in my life. Looking back, I realize that I didn't have a close personal relationship with Him. I thought I was a good Christian though. I even played the organ and piano at church and sang with my sisters for special music. I would go to the nursing home on Sabbath afternoons to sing and visit with the elderly people, but I was far too busy living, working, and studying to spend very much time with my Savior. I thought I could handle things. I thought I knew best. After all, I was eighteen.

I had decided to do things my way. I sailed through my freshman year of nursing at Southern Missionary College, bought my first car, and loved my first real job. Earlier in the year, against my parents' wishes, I'd entered the Miss Kentucky beauty pageant and won both the talent competition and Miss Congeniality. But it was the bathing suit competition, with its infamous walk down the runway, that would come back to haunt me. It was the very part of the pageant that my father was completely against. But I'm getting ahead of my story. All I can say now is that that fateful summer, while I lived with my sister Linda and her husband, I felt very grown up.

One evening, after I'd finished my shift as a student nurse at a small drug and alcohol rehab facility, I slid behind the wheel of my cherry-red 1969 Pontiac LeMans, eager to head home for a good night's sleep. I rolled down the windows and cranked up the volume on the radio. A warm summer breeze blew a lock of my shoulder-length, light brown hair about my face as I eased my "baby" out of the parking lot onto the empty street in Crestwood, Kentucky. Brushing the lock aside, I harmonized with the pop vocalist on the radio. I glanced at the clock on the dashboard—12:30 A.M. Fifteen minutes and I'd be home.

I'd been working double shifts, covering for a night nurse whose attendance was spotty at best. On the nights she didn't show, I couldn't leave the floor until the morning nurse arrived. When I complained to my supervisor, she explained that the nurse had personal problems and asked me to be patient. After a few weeks, even though I was exhausted, I was unable to fall asleep once I got home. When I told my supervisor of my problem, she went to her office and returned with a bottle of pills called Quaaludes.

"Take one or two of these immediately before leaving work. And by the time you get home, you'll sleep like a baby."

I'd never before taken any pills to make me sleep, but I trusted her. She was not only a nurse but also my supervisor; I figured she ought to know. I had completed only one year of nursing school, which had not included pharmacology. I had gone to Christian schools, and even though I was in the midst of the "hippie" days of drugs, I had remained totally untouched by it. In fact I had never heard about illegal drugs, much less been offered them. It never occurred to me that taking prescription drugs without a prescription was illegal. I was just grateful that my supervisor had something to help me.

I took the pills as she said, and it worked for a couple of weeks. But soon my body grew tolerant of the medication, and I needed to increase the dosage to acquire the same effect. On this particular night, the pills I'd taken were already weaving their dreamy cocoon of sleepiness in my brain when I exited the parking lot.

Zipping along the empty, tree-lined street, I tapped my fingers on the steering wheel. Not a soul was about; not another automobile drove past. Only the headlights from my vehicle pierced the mantle of darkness in the sleepy Southern town.

As I approached a stop sign, I slowed down and looked both ways. Since no one was around, I rolled through the intersection. My foot had barely touched the accelerator when blue lights flashed in my rearview mirror. My heart sank.

"Great! This is all I need—a traffic ticket." I sighed and eased to a stop beside the road. Once I'd shifted the car into park, I removed my driver's license from my wallet and looked around. *Where had this guy been hiding? How had I missed seeing him?* The police car's headlights reduced my view of the approaching patrolman to a giant shadowy figure.

The officer bent his six-foot-four-inch frame down and peered into my car. A wide grin filled his strikingly handsome face. *Whoa! What a hunk! This is definitely encouraging.*

"Did you see that stop sign back there?" His voice oozed with charm.

"Er, yes sir." I batted my eyelashes and smiled helplessly up into his face.

"Miss, I need to see your driver's license and registration, please."

"Yes, officer." I handed him my license and retrieved my registration from the glove compartment. I silently watched as he examined the documents.

"Hmm, a Tennessee license—Collegedale." His friendly demeanor gave me courage. Perhaps there was hope. "Are you a student?"

"Yes, sir. I'm studying nursing at Southern Missionary College. During the summer I'm living with my sister and working at the drug rehab." I gestured in the direction from whence I'd come.

As he handed my license and registration back to me he flashed me a gigantic smile. "Well, I couldn't possibly give you a ticket, you being my neighbor and all."

"Neighbor?" I blinked in surprise.

"Yep. I live across the hall from your sister's apartment. I've seen you going in and out of her place all summer."

"Really?" I was flattered that he remembered me.

"Yeah. Maybe we could date sometime. How about dinner Saturday night?"

I wasn't in the habit of dating strangers, and I knew it wasn't a good idea to date someone who wasn't a church member. But what's the harm of dating a guy that wasn't a member of my church—after all it was just one date! It wasn't like I was going to marry the guy or anything! I thought for a moment. *The man is my neighbor, and he did let me out of a ticket. Who's safer to date than a policeman? And he's so-o-o cute.* I'd been working such long hours at the rehab. I quickly convinced myself that I deserved a break. "Sure. I'd love to go out with you on Saturday night."

"Terrific! I'll pick you up at seven." He flashed me another smile.

"Seven it is." I tipped my head to one side and smiled coyly.

"Drive carefully, you hear. It isn't safe for young girls like you to be out at this hour."

"Thanks. I will. Oh, I didn't catch your name."

"Dave. Dave Logan."[1]

"OK, Dave. See you Saturday night." I drove home, parked the car, and floated into Linda's silent apartment. Tossing my car keys onto the dresser in my room, I prepared for bed. I felt very pleased with myself as I drifted off to sleep.

On Saturday night Dave arrived at my door looking more dashing than I'd remembered, and, oh, so charming. He took me to a quaint little Italian restaurant, complete with red-checkered tablecloths, wine

The Pontiac LeMans Brenda was driving the night she met her future husband.

bottles for candleholders, and a fire crackling in the hearth, though it was midsummer. As we followed the maitre d' to our table, the women in the room stared openly at my handsome escort. Even the waitress couldn't stop staring long enough to make eye contact with me as I placed my order. Flattered that Dave was interested in me, I basked in the attention.

On the way home, he drove in silence while I bounced from topic to topic in a typical eighteen-year-old fashion, chatting about my work, my studies, my love of music, and my family. Parking his car outside our

---

1. Dave Logan is a pseudonym.

apartment house, he turned off the engine and looked soulfully into my eyes. I'd dated enough in high school and college to know that this was the moment in the evening where I had to take control of the situation. With a light-hearted enthusiasm I assured him I'd had an absolutely delightful evening. Instead of immediately hopping out of the car as I knew I should, I lingered.

He smiled, then draped his arm across the back of the car seat and trailed his fingers along the line between my blouse and my neck. The mere thought of this man holding me in his arms and kissing me sent tingles of excitement up and down my spine. Reluctantly I placed my right hand on the door handle, preparing to exit. I whispered, "I've got to go."

"Wait." His eyes softened. "Brenda, I think I'm falling in love with you."

I laughed nervously. "In love? You don't even know me."

"I know you enough." He inched across the seat until I could feel his breath on my face.

Why can't I think of something wise or clever to say? He can't be serious. I searched his face for the hint of a smile. There was none.

He twirled a lock of my hair around his finger. "Spend the night with me. Maybe by morning you'll love me too."

"Listen, Dave, I'm not the kind of girl who goes in for that sort of relationship. I'm a Christian. I believe that sex was sanctioned by God. And He designed it to be between two married people." I noted the look of confusion on his face. "Long ago I vowed to save myself for the man I would one day marry."

His mouth dropped open; he drew back in surprise. "Are you saying you're a virgin?"

"Absolutely." I couldn't hide the note of pride creeping into my voice. Some of my college friends had long since lost all pretense of purity. At school I sometimes felt like Elijah when he lamented to God how all of Israel had bowed their knees to Baal. Dave stared incredulously at me, as if I were a mutating specimen in a Petri dish.

"I want to wait until marriage because I believe that when two people have sex outside of marriage, they are married in God's eyes, whether or not there is a legal document to prove it."

"You've got to be kidding!" His burst of laughter filled the car. He pounded the steering wheel with the palm of one hand and shook his head as he laughed. "I can't believe it!" He got out of the car, came around, and opened my door. As he took my hand and helped me to my feet, he gently kissed me on the cheek. "Strange as it may sound, you've made me want you all the more."

Concerned that he might not understand how important my views were to me, I hastened to assure him. "I am serious about this."

He laughed again and gave me a brotherly hug. "Don't worry, princess. I like you enough. I will respect your wishes."

Several nights later I came home from work after midnight. My body had become so accustomed to the sleeping pill routine that I had taken three before leaving the rehab. As I eased into the apartment building parking lot, Dave's patrol car pulled up beside me. He leaped out of his car and dashed to the driver's side of mine.

"Brenda!" He flashed me a disarming smile. "I just got the latest Doobie Brothers album. You've got to hear them! They're fabulous."

I wrinkled my forehead in consternation. "Who are the Doobie Brothers?"

"You never heard of the Doobie Brothers?" If a flying saucer had landed in the parking lot beside his patrol car he couldn't have been more surprised. "Where have you been living?"

I laughed. "I'm afraid I grew up listening to religious music. We didn't even have a television in our house. Dad calls it 'devil-vision.' He felt the same way about the devil's music."

Again Dave shook his head in disbelief. "Well, ya gotta hear them. Come on, you'll love them." He guided me from the car.

Though the pills I'd taken were beginning to spin their magic, I allowed his enthusiasm to overpower my craving for sleep. "OK, just for a few minutes. But I really do need to get some sleep."

As we walked toward his apartment, he told me about someone he'd pulled over that day for speeding. "You wouldn't believe the excuses this guy made." He laughed and recited a few of them. "I think I've heard them all."

He paused to unlock his apartment door and turn on the lights and then gestured toward the open door. "Come on in."

I stepped inside and glanced about the neatly kept room, hardly the typical bachelor pad. I was pleasantly surprised.

"Make yourself comfortable." He strode to the stereo and put on the album. I sat down on the sofa and leaned back to listen to the music. The phone rang. He picked it up and spoke in low tones. Covering the mouthpiece with his hands, he said, "This is police business. I have to take it in the other room."

I stood up. "Maybe I should go. We can do this tomorrow."

He gently took my arm. "No. Please don't go; it will only take a minute. I'll be right back."

As I think back on that pivotal moment in my life, I've asked myself hundreds of times, why didn't I leave? I had the opportunity—he was on the phone, and I was dead tired! I knew the dangers of being alone in a strange man's apartment, especially at that time of the night. Yet, the devil had set me up to fall into his trap by dulling my mind with drugs and then dangling in front of me a handsome hunk who lured me into his apartment. I fell hook, line, and sinker.

So, instead of doing what I knew I should, reluctantly I agreed to stay. As pleasant as the music was, all I really wanted was to sleep. I sat down again on his couch to wait for him.

The next thing I knew, light from a window was shining in my face. I started in surprise. One quick gaze about the room, and I realized I was in a strange bedroom. Stupefied, I glanced at Dave's sleeping form beside me. His clothes lay strewn across the floor, and I could see mine draped on a chair on the far side of the room. What had I done? I was devastated beyond words. I had no memory of anything after sitting down on the couch to wait for Dave to finish his phone call.

Filled with shame and horror, I burst into uncontrollable tears. I cried so hard that the bed shook. This awakened him.

"What? What's wrong?"

I couldn't speak. All I could do was sob.

"Why in the world are you crying?" He drew me into his arms. "Last night was absolutely wonderful. You sure weren't crying then." He gave a meaningful snicker, which reduced me to another bout of tears. "Come on, don't be upset. You were the one who wanted it!"

I pushed him away, gathered the sheet about my body and turned away from him.

He continued, "Is this about that virgin thing in the Bible? Well, don't worry. I'll do the right thing by you. I'll marry you."

At the mention of marriage, I wailed again. How could I marry this stranger? We'd only dated one time. I didn't know anything about him. *Yet,* I wondered, *do I have a choice? In God's eyes we're married anyway!*

I grabbed my clothes and ran into the bathroom. From outside the door, he continued to comfort me with promises of making an honest woman out of me. I dressed as quickly as I could and then waited until I saw my sister's car leave the parking lot. She wouldn't think anything about my not being home overnight because of my crazy work schedule. As soon as I was certain the coast was clear, I dashed across the hall and made a beeline for her bathroom. Dave ran after me, banging on Linda's apartment door that I'd slammed behind me. Locking the bathroom door as well, I vomited into the toilet. I continued to vomit until I had only dry heaves. I felt weak all over when I staggered to my feet and stepped into the shower.

Guilt washed over me. If only I hadn't gone to his apartment. If only I hadn't taken the sleeping pills. I could hear my father's voice: "The wages of sin is death." I wished I could die. That would be the easy way out!

"Lord, what have I done? This has to be a nightmare. Make it stop! Please, make it stop!" Feeling filthy and dirty, I scrubbed and scrubbed until my body was raw and sore. Yet I still felt unclean. I dried off, stumbled to my bedroom, and threw myself onto my bed. I sobbed until I had no more tears. Sliding to my knees, I pleaded with God to forgive me, to take my life.

My head ached from the medication's hangover. My mouth felt like I'd swallowed a handful of cotton balls. If only I could think straight! If I married him, would I finish my nurse's training? I'd wanted to be a nurse for as long as I could remember. When I told my parents, what would they say? What about the warnings in Scripture about marrying a nonbeliever? Could I deny God's commands? Was there no other way?

By the time I arose from my knees, I knew what I would have to do. I would marry this man. I would pray that God would fill my heart with love for him. And maybe, just maybe, it would work out.

Today, I realize that we always have a choice. Two wrongs never make a right. Even though I prayed, I didn't listen for God's answer, and I was about to make the biggest mistake of my life!

CHAPTER 2

A Death Sentence

I dressed slowly, layer by layer, hoping to hide my shame. Before the mirror, as I combed the snarls out of my hair, I could barely look at the reflection of myself. It seemed as though I were staring into the face of a stranger. Disgusted at the mere sight of me in the mirror, I was over-come with guilt and shame. Dave's taunting words, "Come on, don't be upset, you were the one who wanted it," kept ringing in my ears! How could I have been so stupid!

I tried to reason. *Dave was a policeman. He would never have gone to bed with me if I had not wanted it, so it must have been my fault!* Of course I thought he was handsome, but I never once thought of sleeping with him! *What is wrong with me? Why in the world did I even accept that first date, and why did I take those stupid sleeping pills? Why can't I remember what happened? And now I am no longer a virgin! No man would ever want me now. I might as well get it over with,* I thought. *In God's eyes I am married anyway!*

With steps of dread I crossed the corridor between the two apart-ments and knocked on Dave's door. He opened the door as though he'd been expecting me. One look and he drew me into his arms. I didn't hug him back. I couldn't. It was all I could do just to be near him and not run for the toilet and vomit all over again. How strange that a man so hand-some just the day before was so repulsive to me today. I wished that this was all a bad dream and I would wake up. Stepping away from him, I took a deep, agonizing breath. "I accept your offer of marriage—the sooner, the better."

"That's great! Do you want a wedding with the church, and gown, and all that stuff?"

"No. The justice of the peace will do."

"Even better! It's cheaper that way." Still delighted with the fresh turn of events, he strode from the room. "Let me get a calendar. We can pick a date."

I crossed the threshold into his apartment. The door swung closed behind me with a thud of finality. I couldn't believe I was doing this. I remained standing by the door until he returned.

"Here! How about in two weeks? I can take time off from my job so we can have a weekend honeymoon at least."

A honeymoon! The words cut me to the quick. This should be the happiest moment of my life. I should be jumping into his arms, ecstatic about marrying the man of my dreams. Instead I felt numb, as if I were negotiating a business agreement. No, more like standing in a courtroom receiving a death sentence.

"I want you to meet my folks right away," he continued. "They live close by."

Folks? I caught my breath. By now my somber attitude had affected his.

"Tomorrow night. Would that be a good time for you?"

I nodded, trancelike. This farce of a marriage would affect so many people. Speaking of parents, how would I suddenly announce to my parents that I was getting married? I eyed him thoughtfully. How could I convince them that I was in love with this man? How could I convince myself?

I called in sick for work on the evening I made the fateful phone call to my parents in Fall River, Wisconsin. And it was true; I'd never felt so sick in my life. The apartment was quiet. Linda, her husband, and their son had gone to his uncle Cal's for the evening. They wouldn't be back for some time. I hesitated before picking up the receiver to place the call. *How am I going to do this?* I took a deep breath and dialed their number.

When I heard my mother's voice on the other end, I almost broke down. Taking another deep breath, I conjured up as much excitement as I could. "Is Dad home?"

"Yes . . ." She sounded cautious.

"Tell him to get on the extension. I have some wonderful news for you." I nibbled on a fingernail as I waited for my father to pick up the extension.

"Brenda? What's going on?" My breath caught in my throat at the sound of his voice. *This is going to be harder than I thought.*

"Are you both sitting down? You need to sit down." I squeezed my eyes shut and bit my lower lip while I gave them time to get seated. "Mom, Dad, I have met the most incredible man and we're getting married in two weeks! Isn't that exciting?" Silence followed. "Hello? Are you there?"

My father answered. "Yes, we're here. But I don't think I heard you right. What are you talking about?"

"Oh, you're going to love Dave. He's the most handsome man I've ever met. He's a Kentucky state trooper. He's thirty years old. Twelve years older isn't so much, Dad. And he has a daughter from a previous marriage. Her name is Michelle, and she's adorable." I prayed that my barrage of information would keep my breaking heart from giving itself away.

"Is he a Seventh-day Adventist?" Dad's words were slow and deliberate.

"No, but I'm sure that once he knows the truth he will be. You wait; you'll see."

"Oh, Brenda, please don't do this." I could hear the agony in my mother's voice. My mother understood pain. At sixteen she'd come home from school to find police swarming through her home and her parents' blood all over the dining-room floor. Her father had put a bullet through her mother's head and then killed himself.

How I hated causing her more suffering. But I couldn't see any other way out of this situation. Beyond it all, I had to get married, because in God's eyes I was already married. When I heard my father let out a sob, I dissolved into tears. *Oh what have I done!* I could remember as a child Dad telling me that one lie will lead to another lie. It wasn't bad enough that I had lost my virginity to a total stranger, but now I was lying to my parents to cover it up!

If I had been honest with my parents at this point, they could have explained to me that two wrongs don't make something right. My dad may have even reminded me of God's willingness to forgive the woman caught in adultery, so certainly He would forgive me. Perhaps my folks could have persuaded me to turn from the foolish, irresponsible path I was pursuing. If only Jesus was in control of my life, I wouldn't have been in this mess!

"Please, Brenda, don't do it. Wait a year at least! Give yourself time to get to know him better."

"No. No, I have to do this."

"Are you pregnant?" My mother's question cut through me like a knife.

"Absolutely not!" How could they think such a thing? In high school and college I'd had many boyfriends, but I'd never as much as shared a long kiss with them. When a boy tried to persuade me to go too far, I broke off the relationship immediately. There were girls in academy who would "sleep around," and I was well aware of how they were talked about as "cheap" and were called names befitting a streetwalker. I determined that I would never be like that and my virginity was to be protected at all cost! I was proud of the stand I had taken and didn't want anything to damage my reputation.

Now here I was in the worst possible situation. Even though I knew this was hurting my parents, I knew in my heart that telling them the truth would hurt them much more. *I cannot and will not hurt them anymore. I love them too much. I will not bring shame upon them. Stick to the story,* I scolded myself. *After all, I am the one stupid enough to make this horrible mistake. I must live with the consequences. Besides, I can't bear to see the look of pain and disappointment on their faces if they only knew! What would they think of me?*

Mom continued. "You're not making any sense, honey. Please help us understand why you would up and marry a thirty-year-old divorced man whom you've just met. And in only two weeks? Brenda, be reasonable."

Because I was too embarrassed to level with them, nothing I said made sense. I knew they were disappointed and confused when I hung up, but I had to stick to the plan. I couldn't tell them the truth of what I'd done. To tell them I'd sinned before God with this man was far worse.

The next person I had to tell was Linda, which would be harder because I would have to tell her in person. *Oh, Dad was so right. One lie just leads to another lie. Will the lies ever stop?* As I prepared to deliver my "great" news, I tried to paste a delighted smile on my face. But we were close, and I knew she could see right through it.

"Linda, I've met an absolutely gorgeous man, and in two weeks we're getting married."

"What?"

I hurried on. "You know him—Dave, from across the hall. He asked me to marry him this morning, and I agreed."

"Brenda, is this a joke? You're not serious!"

"Yes, I am. This is for real!"

"You hardly know the man. Why, I've barely met him myself, and I've been living across the hall from him for months. You can't be serious."

"I am serious. We've set the date and everything."

My sister shook her head in disbelief. "Well, dates can be unset."

I exhaled slowly. "No, this one can't. Sorry, I know you're disappointed, but this is just the way it is."

"Have you told Mom and Dad yet?"

I dropped my head. "I called them earlier. Tomorrow I'm going to meet Dave's parents. They live here in town."

"How can you marry him? Think about what you're doing."

I tightened my lips in defiance. "I know what I'm doing. You can't talk me out of it."

Devastated, she begged me not to go through with what she called a hare-brained scheme. She wept; she pleaded; she reasoned; she cajoled; she scolded. At one point of weakness, I considered telling her why the marriage had to take place, but I was too embarrassed over my stupidity. On top of everything else, I felt I couldn't cope with the shame I would feel if my family knew. Besides, if I really wanted this arrangement to work, if I really wanted this marriage to succeed, the fewer people who knew the dirty secrets of Dave's and my transgression, the better.

"We're not having a regular wedding, just our vows before the justice of the peace."

"No! No!"

When she saw I was determined on this point as well, she insisted that I at least have a wedding. "You can't get married in front of a justice of the peace. You need a church wedding. Look, I'll talk with Jim's mom and his Aunt Mazie. I'm sure they'll want to help me give you a proper wedding."

"Linda, I don't want to get married in a church!" I was emphatic.

She shot me a curious glance. "OK, OK. Let me work on it, and I'll get back to you. But you are not, do you understand, you are not getting married before a justice of the peace!"

Before I realized it I was trapped in an avalanche of wedding plans. A friend of Linda's offered to let us hold the wedding ceremony in her home. Later that night I called my parents to invite them to the ceremony.

"No!" My father was adamant. Try as she might, my mother couldn't change his mind. "I cannot support your decision to marry this man in such haste. No, I'm sorry, but we will not be there. I cannot be a part of this!"

At his announcement I could hardly breathe. *My father not attend my wedding?* If only I didn't need to be there myself. Trying to ease the trauma of having my parents refuse to attend the wedding, Linda pushed me for information. "What colors would you like?"

I shrugged. "I don't care."

"Have you thought about your wedding dress?"

"Not really."

"We can go shopping tomorrow—"

"No, I don't want to spend the money."

"What about music? Have you thought about that?"

"Look, anything you want is fine with me. I don't really care." I padded off to my bedroom.

As I lay on the bed staring up at the ceiling, I recalled the fun times my two sisters and I had playing "wedding," our favorite game of make-believe. At night we would lie in bed and plan our weddings. We would make up funny names for the men we'd marry and shriek with laughter.

Once Dad brought home some calves. He believed it was good for our characters for us to get up at five o'clock every morning and feed them and help clean out the barn each night. As a result, when we imagined ourselves marrying a doctor or dentist or pastor, we would tease one another by saying that the other sister would marry a farmer and end up raising cows. We'd had fun planning every detail of our weddings and the extravagant receptions. And now, when the event was about to actually happen, I couldn't care less. I felt numb, like a body stripped of its spirit.

The next morning at breakfast, Linda asked, "Will you, at least, wear my wedding dress?"

I shrugged again. "Sure. Sounds fine."

The evening I met Dave's parents was a night I would never forget. The old saying of "how a man treats his mother is how he will treat his wife" should have sent me scrambling for the exit. But I was committed. I'd never run from a challenge in my life, and somehow I knew that I'd face this one with the same determination as I'd used in the past.

If only I had relied on God. If only I had asked Him what I should do. If only I had done what Ellen White says to do in her book *Messages to Young People,* that if you are thinking of getting married, pray twice as much as you ever did before. Instead, I was too embarrassed to even pray—and I stubbornly decided to get out of this mess my own way!

Dave's father worked for the Louisville Medical Association, and his mother was a licensed practical nurse. Neither parent had strong objections to our wedding plans. In fact, they seemed very supportive. This was encouraging, as I was still smarting over my own parents' reaction.

During the course of the evening, an argument broke out between Dave and his father. What it was about, I don't remember. I sat on the sofa, frozen with fear while the two men screamed at one another. I'd never seen two people so angry or out of control. By the time Dave's father stormed from the room, his mother was crying and yelling at her son. Suddenly Dave picked up the telephone off the end table, ripped the cord from the wall and hurled the phone across the room at his mother. In the nick of time, she ducked. The telephone crashed against the wall behind her head. When I started to speak, he turned his rage on me. "Shut the ——— up!"

Like a beaten puppy, I followed him from the house to his car. We didn't speak during the short ride back to the apartment. When I got to the building I bolted for my sister's place. Fortunately no one was home. I ran directly to my room and threw myself onto my bed and sobbed. "Oh God, how can I go through with this? How can I spend the rest of my life with this man? I'd rather die. Please let me die!"

I had no way of knowing then that my desperate prayer was the first of many such prayers and the beginning of my real relationship with God. I had simply acquired knowledge about God before. I should have prayed, "God, should I go through with this?" But instead I prayed a selfish prayer to almost "bless" the foolish path I had decided to take—without the counsel of anyone. My only request for God was that He get me out of trouble by letting me die. Sometimes God allows us to be brought to our knees so that we realize our need for total dependence on Him.

The wedding took place as planned. Linda and her friends had decorated the house beautifully. I listened as I was told that I would descend the winding staircase to meet my intended. "You've got to make a grand entrance," Linda had said, trying to evoke a note of enthusiasm from me. But what did I care about a grand entrance?

There were wedding napkins with our names imprinted on them and light refreshments to follow the ceremony. As Linda and the other women took me through the decorated parlor, I tried to act pleased, but an overwhelming sadness permeated my entire being. Several times I almost broke down but instead bit my lower lip and continued with the farce.

Much to my surprise, my parents arrived two hours before the ceremony. Mom had talked Dad into coming despite his reservations. "She is still our daughter, and we should be there," she'd said.

I was shocked that Dad relented. When Linda told me of their arrival, I ran to my father. I tried to give him a hug, but he stood stone stiff. Since I was a toddler I could always run into his open, accepting arms. It was the most devastating moment of my entire life. I had always prided myself as being "daddy's little girl."

My mind flashed back to the day I left home to attend Georgia-Cumberland Academy in north Georgia. Although there were several boarding academies closer to our home in Wisconsin, I wanted people to know me for myself rather than following in my older sister's footsteps. When my parents took me to the airport, Dad hugged me so tightly I couldn't breathe. It seemed as though he never wanted to let me go. I could see that he was struggling to hold back tears. His words rang in my ears, not only on the plane ride to Georgia but every day since. "Bibby [his nickname for me], I love you so much, more than anything. I want us to be in heaven as a family. Make me proud! Most of all, make Jesus proud of you." Now I had not only let Daddy down but also disgraced my heavenly Father.

How far was God going to let me go? How much trouble was He going to let me get myself into in order for my prideful, selfish spirit to be broken so that I would finally learn that I couldn't do it myself and would humbly and totally rely on Him for everything?

On my wedding day I didn't hear the beloved nickname come from my father's tightly pressed lips. My shame kept me from making eye contact. I don't know what I said to him, but I fled to the upstairs bedroom where I was to dress for the wedding. I'd barely closed the door behind me and had thrown myself onto the bed when I heard someone knocking on the door.

"Who is it?" My words came out in sobs.

"Linda. May I come in?"

"Yes, I-I-I guess so." I reached for a tissue from the brass filigree box on a nearby nightstand and blew my nose.

She opened the door and scooped me into her arms. "Oh, Brenda, I am so sorry . . ."

"He wouldn't even hug me . . ." I dissolved into another bout of tears.

"What did you expect? This wedding is a lot for him and Mom to take. Give Dad time, honey. He loves you so much. Just give him time."

CHAPTER 3

To Love, Honor, and Obey

My sister's Chantilly lace-covered, white satin wedding gown fit my body as though it had been designed especially for me. The gathered, full-length skirt swirled gracefully atop a wide hoop slip. I stared unbelievingly at my reflection in the mirror. The veil and the tiara of pearls should have made me feel like a princess. Yet I felt anything but royal. I wasn't a little girl playing bride. This was for real!

Like most sisters, we had borrowed clothes ever since we were kids. But I never imagined I would be wearing a borrowed gown on my wedding day, and that day I didn't care. My mom sniffled into a tissue while I stood, patiently disinterested, as my sister fastened the long row of tiny satin buttons up the back of the gown. Linda, my only bridesmaid, wore a mint green bridesmaid dress I'd worn for a friend's wedding a few months previously. I barely noticed how lovely my mother looked in the light-green gown she'd borrowed from a friend. I felt like a casual observer at a wedding for someone else, not for me.

Only a handful of people came to the ceremony. My sister Cinda lit the candles. My brother Kenny looked solemn in his dark suit and polished shoes. My brother Jimmy was visiting a friend when my parents decided at the last minute to attend the wedding, so he couldn't be there. Linda's in-laws, Sherry and Aggie, attended as well as Jim's uncle Cal and aunt Mazie, who had helped with the wedding preparations. Kim and Ross, the cousins of Linda's husband, Jim, attended too. Ross's wife, Janean, played the piano, while Jim's aunt Tootsie sang. As a person who loves music, I find it ironic that I can't remember what song she sang at the wedding or even the name of the preacher who married us.

Brenda dressed in Linda's wedding dress on the day she married Dave Logan.

As I descended the staircase, Dave gazed up at me with the charm and devotion expected of a nervous bridegroom. His parents, his only brother Jeff, and a few of his police buddies looked delighted, while pain and sadness filled my family members' faces.

* * *

I can't remember where we went for our honeymoon. Did we drive for hours or for just a short time? I couldn't tell you. Did he take me to a cozy cottage or a hotel room? I don't know. My mind has blocked most of the details of the trauma of my wedding night from my memory.

Imagine marrying a man because you believe you've had sex, and in God's eyes you are already married, only to discover on your wedding night that you had not broken God's commandment and that you had been a virgin all along. What an idiot! How stupid! How duped! I felt like the biggest fool alive. As the truth of my error sank in, I burst into tears. Once I started crying, I couldn't stop.

As for Dave, he collapsed onto the bed with laughter. "You idiot! How could you be so stupid not to know we didn't have sex that night?" He could barely speak; his stomach hurt so much from laughing. "I thought you were pretending not to remember to ease your conscience or something."

Hysterical, I ran for the bathroom, where I vomited into the toilet bowl. He followed me, laughing and calling me every vile and stupid name he could imagine. "You are, by far, the most stupid _____ I've ever met in my entire life!"

Crumpled on the floor of the bathroom, I sobbed between hiccoughs. "Why did you let me think we'd made love? Why did you want to marry me so badly?"

He snickered as he admired himself in the mirror. "Hey, I decided I would marry you months ago."

"Months ago? That's not possible." I was baffled. "You didn't even know me then."

"Sure I did. Remember the Miss Kentucky pageant you were in last year? I was assigned to the security detail for the pageant." He snorted with pride. "When you walked down the runway in the bathing suit competition, I told my buddies that I was going to date you. When they laughed and said I couldn't get a date with you, I bet them twenty dollars that I would not only date you but marry you."

Suddenly I understood why his police sergeant handed him twenty dollars at our wedding reception. I also recalled the good laugh he and his friends had around the punch bowl. And now, for a twenty-dollar bet I was this man's wife for life. He went on to tell me how he'd purposely rented the apartment across the hall from my sister's place as part of his elaborate scheme to win the bet. My head pounded; I couldn't think straight. I ached from head to toe. Most of all, my spirit was crushed beneath his callous heel. Could my nightmare get any worse?

"You are such an unbelievable dope! I'm going to bed! You coming?"

"Wait just a minute. I need to know something. I need to know why you didn't take advantage of me that first night when you could have done so very easily? What stopped you? I don't understand."

"You are even more stupid than I thought," he sneered. "Do you really think I would risk my badge for you? Not on your life! I wouldn't risk a rape charge. You're just not worth it! What a stupid —— you are!"

"No!" I buried my face in my arms.

He snickered, yawned, and left me weeping on the floor of the bathroom. Closing the door behind him, I lifted my aching body to the side of the tub.

Suddenly, whatever fascination I may have felt for Dave; whatever flicker of hope that I could someday love this stranger, died. Instead, welling up within my heart was an emotion I had never before experienced: HATE!

Yes, I hated this man. How could I be a loving wife to someone when the very sight of him made me vomit? I wept over the dashed dreams of one day marrying a wonderful Christian man who loved God and me with his whole heart. I thought of how everyone had told me that because I sang and played the piano, I should marry an evangelist. We'd make a great team. I laid aside dream after treasured dream as I wept.

Now I had to face reality. I was married "for better or for worse, till death do us part," to a man who not only didn't believe in God but had evil in his heart. One who not only used foul language, had fits of rage, and disrespected his parents and family, but one who had deliberately set out to deceive me so that he could win a twenty-dollar bet—and so he could "legally" use me for his pleasure without being afraid of losing his job.

My mind was racing, trying to make sense of it all. It suddenly hit me that the very first time I met him he had told me that he couldn't give a ticket to his neighbor, that he "lived across the hall from your sister's apartment." How could he have possibly known that I was living with my sister? Right from the very beginning, every move on his part had been calculated and cunning, and I had fallen into the trap he had laid. He was right. I was stupid!

"Oh, God, please let me die!" Once again, a selfish prayer.

I remembered how my father reacted when I told him about entering the beauty pageant. "How can you, a Christian young woman, possibly bring honor to God by participating in a beauty pageant?"

"But Dad, there's a lot of money at stake. If I only place in the top ten, there's the scholarship money." As a pastor, my father had found it difficult to feed, clothe, and educate all five of his children. I reasoned that this was one way I could ease his burdens. I decided that he was being unreasonable and old-fashioned. "It's an awesome opportunity! Besides, it will be fun!"

How bitter that memory now tasted. Whatever attraction I had felt initially for Dave was replaced with repulsion. *If only I hadn't entered the pageant, Dave would never have seen me. And if he'd never seen me, I wouldn't be in this mess. If only I'd listened.* Mom and Dad had no idea of how right they'd been. I should not have been parading about in that pageant, and I definitely should not have been taking those sleeping pills! But oh, how I wished I had some right then, for there was to be no sleep for me.

I watched the night shadows on the bathroom's porcelain walls disappear into the dawn's early light. I wept until there were no tears left to cry. I knew what I had to do. During the long night I'd come to terms with my fate and determined to make the best of a very bad situation. Kneeling on the cold tile floor, I turned my face toward my Source of strength. "Dear Father, I am so sorry for all the stupid things I've done that have led me into to this predicament." I carefully enumerated each of my sins. "Please forgive me. But now that I'm in this mess, help me learn to love this hateful stranger whom I've taken as my husband. From now on, Father, I want to give my heart completely to You."

I recalled the promises of Psalm 23. " 'Though I walk through the valley of the shadow of death, I will fear no evil.' Father, I know that You and You alone can lead me through this dark time. You promised You would never leave me and never forsake me. I claim that promise today as mine."

Dave slept until almost noon. I didn't wake him, but the ringing of the phone did. He was needed for some emergency at work, and after throwing his things quickly into his suitcase, we raced home. My suitcase had never been unpacked. It was almost a week before I saw him again. I was grateful that he called before coming home, giving me time to have a nice supper on the table. I had tried to look attractive for him and had the apartment spotless. While he had been away, I had moved my things from my sister's over to his apartment. It still didn't seem right to say "our apartment," however.

I had added some feminine touches to his bachelor pad, which I could see by the frown on his face were not to his liking. "What the ____ are you doing messing with my place" were his first words to me coming in the door. Hardly the way a new bride would want to be addressed. From that first moment, I took the blame. "I'm sorry. I should have asked you first. I can put my stuff in this closet, would that be OK? I have supper ready for you," I added quickly. I was trying hard to change his sour mood. The meal was eaten in complete silence. In time, I came to prefer it that way.

The one positive thing Dave did for me was to get me off sleeping pills. He didn't do it so much for me, however. It would look bad for the wife of a police officer to be taking illegal prescription sleeping pills and could jeopardize his career. He threw my entire supply away and insisted I quit my job, thus cutting off my supply.

I was awake for four days and four nights and still unable to sleep. Exhausted, I begged and pleaded for just one pill, but he refused. I tried to leave the apartment to get help from the nurse who'd given me the stuff, to see if she'd give me more. When my hand touched the door handle, he grabbed me, slammed me to the ground, and sat on me until I could hardly breathe. He threatened to strangle me to death if I stepped outside the apartment. I had every reason to believe he would. On the fifth day I fell asleep from pure exhaustion. Fear of Dave alone forced me never to take another sleeping pill.

Thus began the marriage that should never have been. The abuse started the first night and stopped only when we were in the presence of others. When we were around family, friends, or even strangers, he would treat me as if I were the most precious person in his life—an Oscar-winning performance! The minute we were alone, all pretense of love evaporated.

I could do nothing to please him. I tried to be kind. He crushed my kindness under his tyrannical boot. I tried to get to know him, but I quickly learned that whenever I asked him about himself or about his childhood, he would fly into a rage. I tried to be the perfect wife and housekeeper. I kept the house spotless, served every meal on time, ironed his shirts, and did everything I could think of to avoid another outburst. That's what I called them—outbursts. If I accidentally left a cabinet door open or if he didn't like something I said on the phone to someone, he would rant and rave about what a useless piece of garbage I was as a wife and as a human being. Whatever was wrong, it was always my fault.

The slightest thing would send him into a rage. At first it was just verbal and emotional abuse. Whenever he spoke to me, he'd begin with vulgar swear words and end his diatribe with a crude synonym for "stupid." "You are so ugly! I never have to worry about you having an affair with another man," he would say. "Who in their right mind would look at you?"

Even now, when someone gives me a compliment on my appearance, I politely say "Thank you" but feel hopelessly ugly inside.

Sometimes he would become so agitated, he would pound his fist through the wall. He kicked his boot through the walls so often that I had trouble hiding the damage. I would hang posters to cover his rage and my shame. It was my shame because I felt that it was my fault that he had gotten mad in the first place. *If I just hadn't provoked him, this never would have happened,* I thought many times. One giant hole in the kitchen wall happened because he was angry that I had not answered the telephone when it rang the first time. I had been washing dishes and my hands were covered in suds. The phone rang twice before I could get to it, and that was enough to send him over the edge. Instantly I knew I had messed up. *If only I hadn't stopped to dry my hands, I could have answered on that first ring! It's all my fault that he kicked the wall in. After all, I know how he hates to hear a ringing phone!*

He ripped the phone from the wall so many times that the telephone company threatened that they wouldn't come out to repair it. However, they did, under a "fix it or else" threat from one of his police buddies.

When Linda visited she would comment on the location of my latest poster. "Isn't that an odd place to hang a poster?" She knew I loved interior decorating and had a flair for it.

"Not really. It's just my style," I would reply. I was becoming expert at covering for Dave's unbridled reign of terror.

This time Linda pulled the poster off the wall, revealing a giant hole in the sheet rock. "What in the world? Brenda, how did this happen?" My sister didn't intend to let me off the hook.

"Hey, it's OK." I snatched the poster from her hands and pressed it back over the hole. "Please leave it alone. Things happen, you know?"

"No, I don't know. You're always making excuses for him. He has no right to treat you this way!"

"Look, I don't want to talk about it. Please go." I fled to the kitchen, where I waited until I heard the front door slam shut.

I was thrilled when Linda's father-in-law arranged to give Dave Bible studies. I prayed that my husband's heart would be changed and he would become the kind and loving husband of my dreams. I knew that Dave always pretended to be interested in the Bible whenever any of my family was around. I thought that with the Holy Spirit's power, anything could happen. In a short time, Linda's father-in-law stopped the studies. I didn't learn until much later that he believed Dave was only feigning an interest.

Linda's husband, Jim, got along well with Dave. Of course, everyone liked Jim. He was quiet and easygoing. The two men would attend games and other local events together. Dave would flash his badge and they would get in free. My husband loved the power that came with his badge.

The time soon came when Dave's verbal and emotional abuse escalated to violence. He had laid down a law that dinner must be ready precisely at 5:00 P.M. and not one minute later, whether he was there to eat it or not. When he was late and his food grew cold, he'd rant because I failed to keep it warm for him.

One night he stormed into the apartment, took one look at the prepared table and screamed, "What's that?" He pointed at the bowl of vegetables. "Green beans? I don't want green beans tonight, I want peas. I told you I wanted peas tonight and green beans tomorrow night! You can't remember the simplest instructions. You are so stupid!"

He escalated into a rage so fast I didn't see it coming. Suddenly he flung me through the air. My body slammed against the wall, my legs hitting the corner of the table before impact. Before I could crawl to my feet, he picked me up under both of my arms and pounded my head against the wall. My ears rang. I was dizzy from the pain. When he dropped me to the floor and reached for the bowl of hot green beans, I scrambled under the table and wrapped my arms about my throbbing head for protection. I

ducked as the bowl of green beans sailed by my head and smashed against the wall behind me. Glass and scalding hot green beans flew in every direction, including all over me. The thought crossed my mind that this would be the end for me. He would indeed kill me.

Brenda, left, pregnant with Becky, sitting with her sister Linda.

To my relief, he stomped out the apartment. The door slammed shut behind him. Seconds passed before I heard his tires squeal out of the parking lot. As I lay on the floor, my mouth bleeding and my head pounding, I wept. *What a terrible failure of a wife I am! He's right. I should have known he wanted peas for supper. Why did I fix green beans? I should have known better. It was my fault. I deserve my punishment.* From then on, everything was my fault, not only in his mind but also in mine.

Two months after our wedding, and the same afternoon he received a long desired promotion as a federal narcotics agent, I learned I was pregnant. Dave was ecstatic. He became somewhat pleasant to me for a short time. For his new post he put away his uniform and grew his hair long. He wore blue jeans and T-shirts in order to look and act like a drug dealer on the street. He would be gone undercover for weeks, leaving me no money for groceries. Remembering all too well the last time I lay on the floor bleeding, I was terrified to ask him for money.

I worried about the health of our developing baby, but I didn't know where to turn for help. Dave and I had recently purchased a new home right next door to Linda and Jim. With my sister and her husband living close by, she would often ask me over to eat when Dave was gone. Sometimes she'd bring by leftover casseroles for me. At the time I didn't realize that whenever she came to visit she would check our cupboards and refrigerator. She knew more than I realized at the time. Her suspicions of Dave were growing.

To help meet my needs, I walked along the streets in town picking up aluminum cans to get a little extra money for food. At the market I would buy groceries that would stretch. I ate a lot of oats, corn meal, and anything else I could find on a super sale.

Everything was top secret with Dave. I never knew when he'd come home. If I needed to contact him, I could only do so through his police sergeant. Whenever he finally did come home he'd be furious if I didn't have food on the table. As a result I made certain that, regardless of his presence or not, I would have a meal on the table at 5:00 P.M. every evening. With every outburst, the violence intensified until I was certain that sooner or later he really would kill me. At first that thought had given me pleasure, but now I had another life to protect.

I treasured the quiet, peaceful days and nights when he wasn't home, though I had no idea at what moment my peace would be shattered. One night my tranquility ended with a phone call.

"Hello?" I held my breath, hoping it wasn't my husband. It wasn't.

"Hello, is this Brenda Logan?" It was a woman's voice. I didn't recognize her.

"You don't know me, but I am calling to tell you that I am in love with your husband. Also I am eight months pregnant, and I am begging you to give him up so we can be together. For the sake of our baby . . ."

Stunned, I gasped, trying to catch my breath. Eight months pregnant? I was eight months pregnant. She'd gotten pregnant about the same time!

I don't know how I got through the rest of the conversation or what was said, but when Dave came home that night I told him about the phone call. This time his outburst terrified me. His words were even more punctuated with filthy expletives.

"I don't want a divorce! I can _____well do as I please. And you shut the _____up about it! Do you understand?" With that he swatted me across the face with the back of his hand, which sent me crashing into the nearest wall. He kicked at me with his boot, leaving dark bruises on my arms and legs.

The next morning my sister popped in for a visit. "Where in the world did you get all those bruises?"

Believing it was the mission of a good wife to protect her husband's name, I lied. "Oh, I'm so clumsy. I didn't bother to turn on the light last night to see where I was going and I ran into the wall. I can be so stupid sometimes." After all, it was always my fault that he got so upset, I reasoned.

"Well, you're sure doing that a lot lately."

I looked away. (I have since learned that even a good Christian woman, who would never lie in any other circumstance, will lie to protect her husband and to avoid more pain.)

She touched my hand. "Sis, you can talk to me."

"No, no, honestly, I am just incredibly clumsy. I guess this baby just throws off my balance or something." I massaged my round belly idly with one hand.

"Are you sure?"

"Linda, I would tell you if anything was wrong, right? I'm just such a klutz."

"OK . . ." She hadn't bought my explanation, but I was relieved she backed off and quit probing.

Two nights later my husband returned home in a violent state of agitation. He screamed in my face as he backed me toward a flight of stairs. "I can't afford to have you keep this kid." The steely glint of rage in his eyes alarmed me. I silently asked the questions I'd asked myself so many times. *Will this be the time he takes my life? What about my baby?*

"Sandra, that ———— [another string of expletives], is threatening to take me to court. If she wins a paternity suit, I could be paying child support for her kid, your kid, and for Michelle as well."

I raised one hand to protect my face and placed the other protectively on my stomach. "No, Dave. No! Please don't hurt our baby . . ." My words came out in a strangled whisper.

One shove by his giant hand against my chest and I felt myself being hurled down the flight of stairs. "No! Oh, God, no!" I shrieked in terror as I tumbled backwards. "Please, dear God, please save my baby!"

CHAPTER 4

Though I Walk Through the Valley

Crumpled in a heap at the base of the stairs, I sensed something was terribly wrong. I struggled to my feet, feeling pain all over. Except for a new battery of bruising on my body, nothing appeared to be broken. Then I sensed sticky moisture. *My baby!* I dashed into the bathroom, leaving a trail of blood as I ran. Once I was safe inside, I slammed the door and locked it behind me. I sobbed uncontrollably. "Oh, dear God, please save my precious baby!"

"Let me in!" The door shook with every pound of Dave's weight. I expected to see his fist break through at any moment. If his barrage of hateful curses could physically penetrate the bathroom's solid-core door, I would have been dead. But the door held.

While I silently screamed, *Go away!* I cowered on the toilet seat knowing every passing moment put my life and the life of my baby in jeopardy. Doubled over from cramps, I rocked back and forth and prayed for my unborn child until Dave stormed from the house. Snatching up my car keys and my purse from the dresser, I drove to my doctor's office.

If the physician suspected foul play, he didn't let on. "Stay off your feet for twenty-four hours. If you haven't gone into labor by then, chances are you won't. Only time will tell."

On the way home, I drove in a daze. Yet as I drove, I gritted my teeth. *It would be so easy to just wander off the road into a concrete embankment. . . . No! My baby!* I prayed to stay conscious and that God would protect the little life growing inside of me. Instead of taking the easy way out, I asked God to increase my faith that He could work things out for His glory.

Dave didn't return home that night. The next day the bleeding stopped. Relieved, I praised God and thanked Him for answering my prayer. God gave me another blessing. Dave didn't return home for three weeks.

He did, however, return in time for our baby's birth. Despite my precarious situation and deteriorating health, I carried my baby full term. After only four hours of labor, Rebecca Lynn was born. I named her after my father's mother, Rebecca Helen. Grandma Helen was proud to have her great-granddaughter named after her.

Holding my beautiful new daughter in my arms, my joy knew no limits. I couldn't remember the pain I'd suffered at the hands of her father. I couldn't feel the lingering bruises over my body. I gently caressed the shock of thick black hair on her head. The nurse who first brought her to me had tied a tiny pink bow in her hair. Like new mothers everywhere, I counted her tiny pink toes and fingers. After thoroughly examining her perfect little body, I felt relief overwhelm me. "Oh, dear God, she's perfect."

For the first time since I'd met my husband, my heart was flooded with happiness. Something happens inside a woman when she becomes a mother. I can't adequately describe it. It's a love so deep that I knew I would give my life for this child without a moment's hesitation. Instinctively I knew that God had blessed me with a baby girl for a reason. A girl would be easier to raise alone than a little boy. Even as I brushed the nagging thought aside, I knew in my heart that sooner or later I would be raising her alone.

When Dave first held Rebecca, he too cried. Hope sprang up in my heart. *Maybe this precious little person will make us a real family.* "Please, God, nothing would make me happier."

But my fantasy was short-lived. On the way home from the hospital he dropped a new bomb. "I'm taking you to your sister's house. I want you to stay there until you can come home and be a proper wife again."

I blinked in surprise. The sneer on his face made his inference clear. To him a "wife" meant only one thing!

"You need to know that I don't want any screaming kid around the house. So you'd better find ways to keep her happy whenever I'm around."

Embarrassed, I knocked on my sister's door and asked if Rebecca and I could stay at her place while I recovered from childbirth. She welcomed me into her home without question. As I look back at this vulnerable time, I believe it was God's way of protecting me—at least for a few days.

During the next couple of days, Linda and I spent many precious hours together enjoying her three-year-old son Jimmy and my new baby. From the start Becky was the best baby you could imagine. She cried only when she was hungry or needed a diaper change. She slept so much, I would occasionally check on her to make certain she was breathing. It was as if God gave her an extra sweet spirit because of our situation.

Four days after her delivery, Dave showed up at Linda's door. He strode into my sister's house as if he owned it. "I've come for my wife and kid."

Linda shook her head and frowned. "Oh, Dave, I don't think that's such a good idea. Brenda is still pretty weak. You know she has von Willebrand's disease, don't you? She lost a lot of blood giving birth. Plus she's up every four hours nursing Becky." Von Willebrand's disease is similar to hemophilia except that the body produces "factor VIII" one time and not the next, while a hemophiliac has a bleeding problem all the time.

"Nope. Get her stuff together. She's coming home with me!"

His disarming smile would have fooled the most discerning observer, but not me. I knew better than to protest or say anything that might inflame him further. Trembling with fear, I sat huddled on the sofa, protecting my child against my breast.

Linda, on the other hand, persisted. "But Dave, Brenda really is too weak to care for Becky alone. She needs my help."

"I'm taking my wife and kid home now!" He snatched up a stuffed teddy bear from the arm of the sofa and tossed it at me. "Brenda, get your stuff!"

Immediately I leaped to my feet and scurried into the guest room where I'd been staying. With one arm I packed Becky's new clothing and blankets into my suitcase. With the other I held my baby close. I could hear Dave and Linda arguing in the parlor. My heart sank when Linda stormed into the bedroom and began stuffing the last of the disposable diapers into a grocery bag. Obviously she'd lost. While she said nothing aloud against my husband, her fury screamed through her every move.

She helped me carry Becky's things back to my place and helped me settle back into bed. It was late evening by the time she settled both of us down for the night. I could tell she was lingering. Tasks that would normally take a couple of minutes took twenty. She was reluctant to leave me alone with my husband. Finally, there was nothing else to do. Becky was asleep in her crib. The diapers were stacked in the diaper changer. My clothes were placed in my dresser.

Before leaving she took my face in her hands and whispered, "If you need me, you call! Do you understand?"

I nodded, fearful that Dave would take out his anger on her. "I'll be fine. Just go." I could barely breathe from the terror inside of me.

When the front door closed behind her, I padded into the bedroom, slipped out of my robe and slid into bed. Before I could pull the blankets protectively over my body, my husband burst into the bedroom. The door slammed against the wall from the force. One look at his face and I was filled with horror as I suddenly realized what he expected of me.

"No! No! Please, no!" My cries fell on deaf ears. The pain was excruciating. "Oh, God, deliver me!" I lost consciousness. Moments later I awakened to an even more intense pain that I could hardly breathe. My stitches from the episiotomy were ripped out! I was hemorrhaging! When the nightmare ended, I stumbled to the bathroom and grabbed a towel. It was immediately soaked with blood.

I staggered out of the bathroom. "Dave, I need to get to the hospital! I'm hemorrhaging! If I don't get a blood transfusion soon, I'll die."

Stretched out on the bed, my husband laughed at me. "I'm not taking you anywhere. Just shut the ——— up!"

My tongue felt thick; my sight blurred. "I'm serious, Dave. I'm losing a terrible amount of blood!"

He uttered an awful stream of swear words. "Shut the ——— up, I said! Can't you understand anything! There's no ———way I'm taking you anywhere!" He snorted. "Besides I'm looking forward to seeing the look of death on your face."

"Becky needs me! She needs a mother. . . ." I stumbled toward my child's bedroom.

"Oh, shut the ——— up! You will die tonight, and I'll give the kid to some foster home to raise."

"Please . . ." I could barely remain on my feet.

"I said shut up, you——!" He slammed his fist across my mouth. I retreated to the bathroom. Determined to remain conscious, I silently prayed. "Oh, dear God, I can't die now. Please spare me, not for me, but for my precious baby. I can't leave her alone in this world with this man!"

My prayer had barely escaped from my swollen lips when we heard a banging on the back door. Dave stopped and looked at me in surprise. Who would be at our door at such an unearthly hour? By now it was almost one o'clock in the morning. He grabbed his bathrobe and stormed into the hallway to answer the door.

"Oh, Linda . . ." He sounded so sincere and so worried.

God had answered my prayer. "Oh, thank You, Jesus. Thank You!" I sobbed and rejoiced all at the same time. God had spared my life. I slumped onto the floor, barely conscious enough to hear the rest of their conversation.

"I'm so glad you came by. I was just going to call you. Brenda fell and hurt herself. She is hemorrhaging. Can you take care of Becky for us while I take her to the emergency room?"

Linda burst into the bathroom. I silently begged her not to ask questions. Fire danced in her eyes as she took in the bloody scene. Without a word she ran to the nursery, scooped up Becky in her arms and a few of her things, and returned for me. "Do you want me to go with you? I could leave the baby with Jim. . . ."

Over her shoulder I could see Dave's threatening glare. Violently I shook my head. "I'll be fine once I get to the hospital."

With Becky safe, I could focus on staying alive. Dave bundled me into his car, set his blue light flashing and turned on his siren for the short drive to the hospital. At the ER he waved his badge around to propel me ahead of the other patients waiting to see the doctors. The attending physician took one look at me and ordered Dave to leave the examination room.

My husband bristled. "I'm not leaving! This is my wife!"

The attending physician's glare equaled Dave's. "I'm not asking you to leave, I am telling you! I don't care if you're a police officer or not. If you don't leave immediately, I'll call security and have you thrown out!"

My husband's eyes blazed with fury. After determining the doctor's unyielding resolve, Dave shot me a "you'd better not say a word" glare and stormed from the room.

Once Dave was gone, the doctor walked to my side and took my hand in his. His eyes shone with tender compassion. I didn't need to tell him anything; he understood. He gazed deeply into my eyes and frowned. "Brenda, I can get you help. You don't have to put up with this."

"I-I-I don't know what you're talking about." I turned my head away. "I just fell and I need you to stop the bleeding. . . ." Even to me my words sounded hollow and unconvincing.

"No! You didn't fall down, you were raped." His words hit me like a lightning bolt. "You need help, and I can help you."

I desperately wanted to accept the protection he offered. I wanted to cry, "Yes, please help me," but I couldn't. I was in the hospital; my baby was at my sister's place. I couldn't risk what he might do to her. "No, I'll be fine. Really, I'll be fine."

I'd lost so much blood that after the physician finished stitching up the damage, he admitted me into the hospital. Before sending the nurse for Dave, he tried one more time to convince me to let him help me. "We have protection for women like you. They'll protect your baby too."

There were tears in his eyes. He might not realize it, but I knew I was different from most battered women. My husband was a police officer. He was the law in our small town. In any legal confrontation, I knew that he would win and I would lose my baby.

Years later, when I tried to retrieve my medical records from the hospital files, they were mysteriously missing. Whether Dave or his father, who worked for the local medical association, paid someone to destroy the doctor's report, I'll never know.

Once more I returned from the hospital to my sister's house. This time I stayed until I was healed. After the emergency room doctor's warning, Dave didn't want any suspicious looking incidents. He would play the doting husband and father whenever he came to visit, almost fooling me if I didn't know him better.

Finally the day came when I had to return home. I feared for my daughter's life. Getting up in the night to be certain she was breathing, I would fall asleep on the floor beside her crib, just in case he came home in a bad mood during the night. The good news was that his work was keeping him away from home for longer periods of time. The bad news was when he did come home he was rarely in a good mood. Not knowing when he'd walk through the door kept me in a constant state of terror.

One day after he came home, I opened the hall closet door to hang up my coat and found two large mailbags on the floor. Curious, I opened one of them. *Marijuana!* I stared in disbelief. Instantly, fear shot through my mind. The last thing I wanted was for him to know what I'd discovered. But before I could reclose the bag, the closet door swung hard against my arm, pinning me between the door and the door jam. I cried out in pain. As he jammed the door against my arm a second time, he swore a string of obscenities at me. "If you say one word to anyone, I'll kill both you and Becky!"

The edge of the door bit into my flesh. With the door holding me fast, he swung his fist at my face. I screamed in pain.

"I didn't see anything. Honest, I didn't see anything!" After a few more blows to my head, he released my arm. Over the next few weeks, mailbags came and went from the closet in the hallway, but I never again opened my mouth or the closet. For Becky's sake I couldn't risk another outburst.

One day when Dave came home he told me that he wanted me to go for a ride with him. He'd done this only once before, during my pregnancy, when he needed a cover-up for a drug bust that was going down. He insisted that I leave Becky with Linda. Terrified I would never again see my child, I kissed her several times before obediently climbing into the car beside him.

As we drove down a country road that seemed to go nowhere I was certain I would die this day. He stopped the car alongside a fenced-in pasture. "Get out of the car and open the gate!"

I obeyed and then climbed back into the car. We drove behind a clump of trees that camouflaged a secluded shooting range where police officers practiced. Pulling his handgun from its holster, he pointed the weapon at me.

"Get out! Go stand in front of the target!"

Dumbfounded, I hesitated, looking first at the target and then at him.

"Get moving, you stupid_____! When I say move, you move!"

I knew I had no choice. I don't know how long I stood in front of the bull's-eye while he fired one shot after another into the target. The explosions of gunfire were deafening. I knew he was a perfect shot and at any moment he could kill me should he choose. Crying and shaking, I begged him to just get it over with. "Just shoot me! Please shoot me!" I pleaded.

My cries sent him into gales of laughter. When he regained his composure, he fired off a string of obscenities and then ordered me back into the car. We rode home without a word. After I got home, I was afraid to put Becky down. I held her all night long, too aware of how close I'd come to never holding her in my arms again.

Becky was barely five months old when I awakened one night to the shocking pain of being jerked out of bed by my hair. A quick glimpse at the clock told me it was three in the morning. My husband's curses rang off the walls of our bedroom. I could smell the distinct odor of alcohol on his breath. My heart pounded in my throat as I struggled to get to my feet. I could hardly breathe. He hauled me across the room by my hair and thrust me through the open bedroom door into our well-lit living room, where three strangers stood. I could tell instantly that the men had been drinking as well. One man, one of Dave's police buddies, held an open beer can in his hand. With nothing on but my nightgown, my husband displayed me like a prize heifer before his friends. "OK, which of you guys wants her first?"

The stupefied, lecherous leers on their faces told me that I would find no sympathy among them. When one of the men swaggered forward to claim his prize, I wriggled free and bolted for the bathroom. The bolt lock slid safely into place a split second before Dave crashed against the door.

"Open this —— door immediately!" He swore and pounded on the door. "If you don't open this door immediately, you ——, you'll be sorry!"

While I didn't doubt that I would eventually suffer his frenzied wrath, I couldn't make myself unlatch the door. I cowered in the corner as he continued to pound his fist on the door. Suddenly he stopped pounding. It grew quiet in the other room—too quiet. I pressed my ear against the door, hoping to pick up any conversation that might be taking place between the men. Then I heard the sound that sent chills throughout my body—my baby wailing right outside the door. My heart stopped.

Over her cries, he laughed. "Guess you'll come out now, you ———!"

I knew I had no choice. I had to do something. The men were soused. Could I use their inebriation to my advantage? If I could grab Becky and escape out the front door, I could run to Linda's place. Bracing myself, I unlocked the door and lunged for my baby. Laughing in my face, he held her high above his head. Frantically I jumped, repeatedly trying to reach her, but at five feet two inches, my height was no match for his superior height and weight.

Suddenly, without warning and still holding her high above his head, he took several long strides to her nursery. I raced after him, still determined to somehow rescue my daughter. At the nursery door, he shot a wicked grin at me and threw her across the room into her crib. I screamed, feeling certain that she would die from the impact. Instead she howled as only an indignant baby can howl. Instantly I knew she hadn't been hurt. *Thank You, God,* I breathed in a silent prayer as I darted past Dave and into the nursery.

As I reached the side of the crib, I felt my head being pulled backward by my hair and I was literally flying across the living room. I could hear my infant daughter screaming, while I felt the impact of his boot, first in my face, then, in my stomach, arms, and legs, until my pain was so intense I could no longer detect where on my body I was being hit. Somewhere in the distance I could hear a man's voice.

"Come on, man, I don't want to be a part of this kind of trouble. Let's get out of here!"

Another of the men agreed. "Yeah, we don't need this ———!"

"Let's go. Come on, Dave, let's get out of here."

This must have sobered him up a bit because with one more kick from his boot, he was gone. I didn't move from my fetal position on the floor as I heard the back door slam and his car drive away. I literally ached from head to toe. There was no spot on my body that didn't hurt. I just wanted to die there on the floor, but my daughter needed me. I knew I had to get out of the house before my husband returned.

CHAPTER 5

Fear No Evil

I crawled to the side of the crib and pulled myself up by the rails. Steadying my quivering legs for a moment, I scooped Becky into my arms. *Maybe if I nurse her she'll quiet down.* Feeling as if my knees might give out on me, I knew running wasn't an option, at least not right away. I lowered myself to the floor. My lips moved automatically as I recited the comforting words of Psalm 23 that I'd learned as a child. "Though I walk through the valley of the shadow of death, I will fear no evil, for Thou art with me. . . ."

I leaned back against the wall and tried to coax her to nurse. Sobbing my heart out, I rocked back and forth, hoping to soothe my baby's jangled nerves. Then I heard the back door close. *Oh, dear God! No! He's come back! Where could we go? Where can we hide?* My mind commanded my legs to flee, but they refused to move.

My panic changed to tears at the sight of Linda standing in the doorway. She was wearing her robe and slippers. *It's after four in the morning! What is she doing here?* I thought. For an instant I wondered if I were imagining her being there. My brain was numb from the trauma of the moment.

Glancing first at me and then at the room, she burst into tears. "This is enough!" She marched to the telephone. I was only faintly aware of my sister's voice as she made plane reservations for me and my daughter. Then I heard her call our parents in Texas.

"Becky and Brenda are coming to visit you today. You need to pick them up at the airport. Here's their flight number." Whatever else she said, I don't remember, for I'd retreated deep within myself.

Knowing Dave could return at any moment and try to stop her from taking me away, she raced through my home, packing a suitcase for me and one for Becky. While Becky heaved soft little sobs as she slept in my arms, Linda cleaned the blood from my face. My two front teeth had been buried in my lower lip. My every muscle ached as she helped me into a loose-fitting dress. By this time I could barely see through my swollen eyes. Within minutes she'd swept us out of the back door, and Jim helped me into their car.

As we sped toward the airport, Linda glanced over the seat and started to panic. "Oh, no! I forgot to put your suitcase in the car! I got Becky's but forgot yours."

Jim jammed his foot down on the accelerator. "I'm not going to risk going back for it. We'll send it to you later. At least we have Becky's suitcase. That's what's important."

On the way to the airport, Linda told me how she came to be in my house at such an unearthly hour. "I awoke out of sound sleep and just knew you were in trouble and that you needed me right away. When I found your back door unlocked, I knew something was terribly wrong; somehow, I knew I'd find you in the nursery."

We pulled into the airport parking lot with only seconds to spare. I could barely move as I climbed out of her car at the almost abandoned airport. With my daughter safe in my sister's arms and her husband keeping me from collapsing, I limped my way to the ticket counter, where Linda secured my ticket. She arranged with the ticket agent to walk with me onto the plane. Through it all, I couldn't stop sobbing.

Once I was safely seated on the plane, she asked the flight attendant to watch over me. "Make sure she gets off the plane in Dallas. Here are my parents' names should she have any trouble in flight."

The flight attendant eyed me sympathetically. After praying a heartfelt prayer that God would go with me, Linda left, and I settled back against the seat for the two-hour flight home. I wasn't cognizant of my surroundings or my condition.

"You are the Great Healer," my sister had said in her prayer. "I am leaving her in the loving arms of Your Son, Jesus."

The attendant hovered nearby, watching over me throughout the flight. When the plane landed and I walked out of the jetway, I saw my father cry for perhaps the third time in my life. Neither he nor my mother was prepared to see me in such a horrid condition. Immediately Mom took Becky while Dad helped me walk to the car. Once he'd seated me inside, he went to the baggage carousel to claim my one piece of luggage. We rode in silence to my folks' home in Mineral Wells.

At the time, my father was pastor of the Mineral Wells, Weatherford, Graham, and Breckenridge Seventh-day Adventist churches in Texas. My folks were wise and knew that my story would come out bit by bit during the weeks and months that would follow. They never said "I told you so" or anything like that. Although they were struggling financially with my two young- est siblings still at home, my folks gladly paid for my plane ticket. I had no money and no access to any. I felt like the prodigal daughter who was given a feast and welcomed home with open arms.

In a tiny three- bedroom parsonage, the arrival of two

Brenda and Becky with her parents and her brother Kenny in Texas.

more people cramped the bedroom space. It was assumed that Becky and I would share my sister Cinda's very small bedroom. That's when my thirteen-year-old brother Kenny touched my heart with his kindness.

"Sis, you and Becky can have my room. I've always wanted to sleep on the sofa, and Mom never lets me." Tears ran down my cheeks at my brother's generous offer. I knew the sacrifice he was making, and I loved him for it.

For the first time in months, I was home. I felt completely safe. A few days later I received a small package of everything that might have sen- timental value to me. I didn't have much. "When we were sure Dave wasn't at home," Linda told me on the telephone that night, "we packed up everything we thought you'd like to keep and mailed it."

"Have you seen Dave?" I was almost afraid to ask for fear he'd try to hurt Linda or Jim.

"He showed up at our door that night in a rage. He wanted to know where my blankety-blank sister was." She paused. "I'd had enough. I told him in no uncertain terms that I'd put you on a plane and sent you home to the folks. I told him you were never, ever coming back again!"

"What did he do?"

"He stared at me in shock. Jim came up behind me. Well, Dave broke down into tears. Jim put his arm around him and let him cry on his shoulder. By the time he left I felt almost sorry for him, so I decided to prepare something for him to eat. When I took the food over to his house, I heard loud music and laughter. He opened the door with a huge grin on his face. How can a man change so quickly? I was shocked."

I wasn't. I'd endured those changes for too long.

"I left the food," she said, "and prayed that God will change this man's wicked heart."

I'd been in Texas for only one month when Dave called.

"Brenda, I am so sorry," he began. "I now know how much I've lost. I've given my heart to Christ and I want to be baptized. Can you possibly find it in your heart to forgive me?"

I shook uncontrollably at the sound of his voice. I couldn't speak.

"I want us to be a real family. I want to be a Christian father to Becky."

To think of going back into that situation terrified me, yet if he really was changed, perhaps we could be a real Christian family. "I-I-I'll pray about it."

When I hung up the phone, I hesitantly told my parents all that he said. They begged and pleaded with me. "No, Brenda! No! Don't even consider going back to him for a moment. Most men like that don't change!"

"But doesn't Becky need a real Christian father?" It was too tempting. A month later Dave moved to Texas. From the start he was very kind, and I so wanted to buy his act. I did think it strange that he wasn't in any hurry to find a job, and he arrived with only one suitcase. When I asked him where the rest of his luggage was, he said, "I'll send for it later."

By this time Becky was eight months old. Dave and I found an inexpensive place to rent. We'd been in the place for six weeks when he announced that he needed to fly to Kentucky to sign some papers. When I returned from taking him to the airport, I discovered that all his things were gone. I knew then that he wasn't coming back. Looking back, I saw that he had given signs and excuses that should have raised warning flags in my mind. But I ignored them because I so wanted our marriage to work out for my daughter's sake.

Immediately I called my mother on the phone. The moment I heard her voice my tears started flowing. "Mama, I think he's gone and not coming back."

Two hours later my telephone rang. It was Dave. He confirmed my suspicions. "Just wanted to let you know I'm not coming back. I had no intention of reconciling with you, you stupid ———— !" He broke into a raucous belly laugh. "You are so ———— stupid! I really got you with that God thing, didn't I?"

How could I have been so gullible? I burst into tears.

"I can't believe you fell for that line. I only came to Texas because my attorney said it was the easiest way to get sole ownership of the house. Six weeks gave me time to transfer the house and my savings to my dad. Now I want a divorce. And don't try to get anything because there's nothing you can get!"

I had no job and no outside source of income. There was nothing I could do but move back home with my parents. Weeks went by and the divorce papers didn't arrive, but I didn't care. At the time I was relieved to just feel safe and loved once again.

I was divorced for several months before I learned the divorce was actually final. My father had handled all the details for me, including a very real warning to Dave. "If you ever try to call Brenda again, or even consider coming near my daughter or my granddaughter, God will not hold me responsible for what I will do to you!"

True to my husband's word, I received no financial settlement, no alimony, and a very small amount of child support. I did receive full custody of Becky, which was the most valuable thing I could hope for. My precious Becky was worth far more to me than any savings account or sale of Kentucky real estate. Even though he wasn't good on paying child support, I didn't complain. I didn't want him to get angry and insist on visitation rights.

At one year old, Becky was diagnosed with gamma globulin anemia, a disease that affects the immune system. She was always sick and in and out of the hospital on a regular basis. On one particular occasion she was placed in intensive care. The doctor told me that her kidneys were shutting down. "If she doesn't have any urine output, she will die! You need to notify her biological father."

"No, I can't!" I recoiled from the very idea of speaking with my ex-husband.

"You don't have a choice!" His stern demeanor shook me out of my lethargy.

Feeling under pressure to do so, I made the call. When I told Dave that Becky was in intensive care and might not make it, he screamed another string of obscenities at me. "Well what the——— are you calling me for? Don't ever call me again unless she is _____ dead!" He slammed down the receiver.

I returned to my daughter's side. As I gazed at the tiny, naked body inside the plastic oxygen tent, struggling for every breath, I determined right then and there I would never call him again—no matter what! I pulled up my chair and slid my arms under the tent so that she could feel me touching her. She was burning up with fever. Though she'd been unresponsive all day, I was certain she could sense my presence. Exhausted, I was afraid I would fall asleep. I wanted to know the instant she had any urine output.

I put my head down on the bed railing and closed my eyes. "Dear Father, please, oh, please, spare my baby's life. You know that she's my only reason for living." I placed my hand under her tiny little bottom and drifted off to sleep. A short time later I awoke with a start. My hand was wet! She had urinated. I was ecstatic.

"Nurse! Hurry! My daughter . . ." My words came as excited garble.

Immediately the nurse called the doctor, who ordered a new series of tests. When the results came in, the doctor shook his head in disbelief. "Your daughter is not only going to live, but she is completely out of danger. Every test came back normal. She can go home now."

"It's a miracle!" I broke into hysterical laughter. "Praise God!" I danced; I cried; I hugged anyone who came into hugging range. Later, cradling my daughter in my arms, I walked past the pay phone in the corridor without hesitation. I'd determined never to tell Dave that our daughter was out of danger. And he never asked.

Life in the Micheff Family

Childhood prints upon our minds and character the pattern of whom we later become. I was a Micheff, and that made a difference in my life. Before moving on to tell you how God truly redeemed me, let me slip back and assure you that before I was battered, I was blessed by being able to grow up in a warm, Christian home where God was very real.

The psalmist could have been looking at my family when he wrote Psalm 128:1–4 (NKJV).

Blessed is every one who fears the LORD,
Who walks in His ways.
When you eat the labor of your hands,
You shall be happy, and it shall be well with you.
Your wife shall be like a fruitful vine
In the very heart of your house,
Your children like olive plants
All around your table.
Behold, thus shall the man be blessed
Who fears the LORD (italics supplied).

CHAPTER 6

A Haven of Safety

Warm Texas sunlight poured into the tiny bedroom that Kenny had so graciously relinquished for my daughter and me. On a sparkling new day I yawned, stretched, and glanced at the clock beside my bed. *Nine o'clock? Becky! My baby! Where's my baby?* I sprang from the bed and ran to the side of her crib. It was empty. *Dave!* At the thought of him, a moment of unreasonable fear became an even more unreasonable terror. Frantic, I threw on my robe and bolted into the hallway. Still fuzzy from the remains of a good night's sleep, I wasn't certain of where I was.

I heard, drifting down the hall from the kitchen, the sound of giggles and laughter—my mother's and my daughter's. Relief flooded through me. I was home; I was safe; Becky was safe in Nana's care! An agonized sob escaped my lips. Instinctively I clamped my hand over my mouth and melted down the hall into a tearful lump of relief. As broken as my spirit was after Dave tried to destroy my life, I was slowly beginning to realize that my circle of family love remained strong.

While I was growing up, my home was always a haven of safety for me. My four siblings and I were raised in a loving Christian environment. During my younger years, my dad sold Christian books door to door during the week and preached on weekends. With five children in the family, keeping food on the table was a struggle. Sometimes he would go for weeks at a time without selling even one book. He joked by saying that we lived on "wonder checks," as in, "I *wonder* where the next one will come from."

My mom maintained a constant and secure presence for us in the home. Raising five kids was a full-time job. The love of God came first and foremost in our lives. And while we often ran short of money— some would consider us poor—we never ran short of love.

During one particularly lean time we were living in Johnston City, Illinois. It was 1958, and I was five years old. There was no money left for groceries, and we children were complaining of being hungry. Dad had us kneel in our prayer circle and hold hands, something we always did in times of trouble, and each of us said a prayer. When my father prayed, he told the Lord how much we loved and trusted Him. "I know You see our need and that You will take care of us, Father."

He'd barely said "Amen" when my sister Linda hopped to her feet and said, "I know how God will answer our prayers, Daddy." She ran to the back door and opened it. We couldn't believe our eyes. On the back porch was as huge cardboard box spilling over with groceries— enough to last for three weeks.

"Look, Mama, oranges!" I squealed in delight. Too expensive for us to buy regularly, oranges were a special treat reserved for Christmas. To this day my parents have no idea who brought the gift to our home.

Sometimes my father would accept unusual gifts in payment for the books he sold. After spending hours giving a Bible study to a potential customer, he would

Micheff family with five kids in West Frankfort.

learn that the person couldn't afford to buy the books. He was more interested in getting the Word of God into the hearts and homes of his customers than he was about getting a paycheck. Over the years he brought home cooking pans, an electric skillet, a vacuum cleaner, a gun, and a horse, to name only a few. He sold the miniature horse to the publishing secretary of the Illinois Conference, who drove it home in his station wagon. People pointed and laughed at the sight of a station wagon passing with a horse's head hanging out a car window.

During one particularly long "dry spell," Dad came across a farmer. While visiting with the man, my father noticed several bags of dried beans on the back porch. Pointing to the sacks, he asked, "What are you going to do with all those beans?"

The farmer gestured offhandedly and said, "Oh, I give them to my hogs."

Hogs? At home our cupboards were bare. My dad attempted to maintain an air of nonchalance. "Would you like me to take a few of those bags off your hands and give them to someone? I know a family who is struggling right now and would probably appreciate them."

The farmer grinned. "Sure, why not? I have so many; my pigs are getting tired of them anyway."

When Dad brought those bags into our kitchen we thought he'd struck gold. There were navy beans, pinto beans, lima beans, and others. Every two months or so, Dad would return to the farm for more beans. For two years beans were the mainstay of our diet. My creative mom cooked those miracle beans in more ways than one could ever imagine. Beyond boiling and baking, she would grind them into flour for pancakes, soups, bean casseroles, and bean sausages. You'd think I would have grown to hate beans, but beans are still one of my favorite foods.

Winter in 1958 was particularly hard for our family. Having no money to pay heating bills, we walked around the house in our winter coats to keep warm. We even slept in coats and boots. When we learned that my mother's brother, Uncle Clifford, and his wife, Aunt Donna, and their new baby were coming for a visit, Dad was really worried for the baby's safety. When our relatives arrived, my father apologized for the lack of heat in the house. They understood because they too were having a hard time financially. My father then invited my uncle to go down to the basement with him.

"I invited you down here so that together we can pray about our problem."

Reluctantly, Uncle Clifford knelt on the cold concrete floor with my father. While my uncle was a Christian, he waffled back and forth in his faith in God. Shivering from the intense cold, Dad placed his hand on the cold furnace. "Lord, You know that I love You. You know that I am doing all I can to serve You. I don't understand why I'm having these financial troubles right now, but Lord, I will continue to serve You no matter what! I don't have the money for heat, and there is a precious infant in the house. If it is Your will, Lord, please start this furnace so this little baby will be protected." With his hand resting on the furnace, Dad said, "Amen."

With a sudden rush and a tremendous roar, the furnace burst to life. Dad, before rising to his feet, added, "Thank You, heavenly Father, for hearing and answering my prayer."

When my father and Uncle Clifford emerged from the basement, my uncle's face was as pale as death. He stumbled to his wife and took her hands. "Donna," he said, "we're not living right. I've just witnessed a miracle!"

The furnace kept running for the next two weeks until my father's paycheck arrived, enabling him to pay for the fuel.

Not being able to afford to continue renting our home in Johnston City, we moved six times that year. At one point our furniture was re-possessed. Finally Mom and Dad found a little three-room home we could afford to rent in Du Quoin, Illinois. We children would sleep on mattresses on the living-room floor.

The tumbledown structure was so infested with gigantic rats that we children would never go into the basement without one of our siblings accompanying us. Every night at worship my father would end his prayer asking God to watch and protect us while we slept. "Please, God, don't let the rats bite my family." He had read an article in a local newspaper about a child who lived not far from us, who'd had her entire ear chewed off by rats. Many nights I awoke to feel a rat running across the top of my blanket. But none ever hurt any of us.

While living in Du Quoin, Dad was asked by the conference if he would consider moving to Centralia. My parents prayed about it and decided to step out in faith. With very little cash and just enough gas to make the forty-five-minute drive north to the town and back, his prayer was simple. "Please, Father, if we are supposed to move to Centralia, let us find a house."

We searched for a house all day long. Toward suppertime, we were getting hungry. "Hey, look!" Mom pointed to a sign up ahead. "It says free ice-cream cones!" A Dairy Queen was offering free ice-cream cones for their grand opening.

"Wow! Can we get some, huh? Can we get some?" We kids squealed with delight. Dad swung our car into the parking lot, parked, ran inside the store and returned with an ice-cream cone for each of us. We silently enjoyed our rare treat while our parents discussed our immediate future. What a grand supper it was!

"It's getting late. I doubt we can see more houses today." Dad peered out of the windshield at the gathering darkness.

Mom dabbed at the melting ice cream dribbling down my little sister Cinda's face. "It doesn't make much sense to use the last of our fuel to drive all the way home and not be able to come back again tomorrow to continue searching for a place."

"You're right. That would be a waste. Maybe there's a park nearby where we could sleep in the car tonight." My father started the car's engine and eased out onto the main thoroughfare.

We'd driven to the far side of town when Mom spotted a city park. Dad drove until he found a secluded parking place next to a picnic table. Mom decided that my younger sister Cinda would sleep in the rear window above the seat. For her blanket, she would use my father's jacket. "Now you two girls," she said to Linda and me, "share the back seat, and, Jimmy, you stretch out on the floor. All three of you will have to share the one blanket I thought to bring with us."

The heavy dew forced my parents to abandon a nearby park bench for the front seat of the car. We'd all settled into a sound sleep when a blinding light shined through our windshield, awakening everyone but Jimmy. A gloved fist banged against the driver's window. Quickly my father rolled down the window.

"Yes, officer?"

The police officer peered into our car. "What are you doing here? Don't you know this is a dangerous place to be?" His raspy growl sent chills up and down my spine.

"What are you talking about, officer?" Dad's voice sounded groggy because he had just awakened from a deep sleep.

The policeman took a step back. "Step out of the car, please."

My father hastened to do as ordered. My sisters and I fearfully huddled together, intent on catching their every word.

"You will have to leave this area. It's not safe," the policeman ordered. "Just last week someone was killed in this park. Now move along."

I saw my dad straighten to his full height. "Officer, don't you think I would like to have my family sleep in a nice motel? I am a servant of God, doing the Lord's work. And I don't know why, but the Lord is testing me right now." My father reached into his pocket and pulled out some change. "I have one dollar and thirty-three cents to my name. I have just enough gas to get home tomorrow. Please let us sleep here tonight. I know the God whom I serve is more powerful than any danger lurking in this park. My God will protect us."

I could tell that the police officer was visibly moved. He cleared his throat and stammered, "Very well, I'll let you sleep here tonight, but lock your doors."

"Yes, sir, I will." Dad shook the officer's hand. We all watched him climb back into his patrol car and leave. Within minutes we'd all returned to sleep, all except for Dad. He stayed awake a while, praying that God would protect us, especially now that he knew of the possible danger. Before he relaxed enough to sleep, my father spotted the patrol car circling through the park. Throughout the rest of the night as we slept, we had our very own uniformed guardian angel.

My most treasured family memories were of morning and evening worships, especially the evening ones when we would all gather around the piano to sing. I cherish the memories of singing "Will the Circle Be Unbroken?" "When the Roll Is Called Up Yonder" and "In the Sweet By and By." We kids would take turns being in charge of the program that followed. We'd play games like Bible charades or Bible tic-tac-toe or twenty questions. Other times we'd choose a Bible character to talk about or a favorite text to discuss. When it was my turn, I spent a long time planning. But as varied as the evening program might be, worship would end with the family kneeling in a circle, holding hands and praying.

Dad was a strong spiritual leader, and Mom totally backed him up. They believed in "Spare the rod; spoil the child." Kenny, the youngest, was the family clown. He always seemed to be in trouble. He wasn't bad, just mischievous. He loved to tease and play jokes on the rest of us.

Once when he had done something he'd been told not to, Dad sent him for the belt. When Kenny returned, Dad told him to bend over and take his punishment.

"But, Daddy, I need to talk to you first."

"I told you to bend over, son."

"Please, Daddy, I really need to talk to you first."

Exasperated, my father sighed. "All right, what is it?"

Kenny looked Dad right in the eye. "Daddy, would Jesus whoop me if He were here?"

My father choked back the urge to laugh. How could he continue with a spanking after that question? Struggling to maintain a serious face, he pointed toward the kitchen. "Kenny, you go to your mother. She will finish the punishment."

As soon as Kenny disappeared from the room, Dad rushed out onto the back porch and burst out laughing. My mother couldn't bring herself to spank him either but sent him to his room for a half hour. Grinning from ear to ear, my clever little brother bounded into his room and closed the door.

While we were sitting with Mom during church, Dad had a warning system he invoked from the pulpit as needed. When one or more of us was whispering or making noise, he would wait until he made eye contact with the offender and hold up one finger as if making a point in the sermon. One finger was a warning; two fingers represented "grace"; and three fingers meant "no grace." Rarely did he need to count to three before we straightened up.

Another memory precious to me was singing with my sisters. We started singing together when Cinda was three, I was five, and Linda was seven. The matching outfits Mom made for us became the "Micheff Sisters" trademark. We sang together almost every Sabbath either at Sabbath School or church, at nursing homes, or on hospital visits to ailing church members. Often, when we sang for one patient, the nurses would request that we sing for another patient who was depressed or who hadn't had any visitors. We were happy to do it. I can understand now that my parents were training us to have a servant's heart and to appreciate the joy of giving to others.

One Friday night when my brother Jim was only four years old, he begged to sing with us. We were practicing our song that we'd sing for church the next morning. Cautiously we agreed to allow Jim, the quietest and shyest of the Micheff clan, to sing with us if he promised to practice and to memorize the words. We'd decided it was important to learn the words so that they came from the heart and not from a page in a hymnal.

The next morning the local elder announced that special music would be presented, not by the Micheff sisters but by the Micheff family. Solemnly we marched up onto the platform and waited for our mom to play the introduction. Jim took one look at the sea of faces before him and panicked. Grabbing my skirt, he buried his head

The Micheff sisters sang for friends, family, and church.

in the fabric throughout the entire song. The audience barely heard what we sang. They were too busy watching our "cute little brother."

Weeks before my eighth Christmas, a church member who was moving away gave us their piano instead of taking it with them. From the moment Dad and a couple of the local church deacons carted the instrument into our home I was mysteriously drawn to it. Mom immediately set down the law. "Children, this is not a toy! No one is to touch it without permission. Do you understand?"

We nodded solemnly. Every chance I got; I would sneak into the living room and gaze at the piano with yearning. I so wanted to touch the ivory keys. The next night while my sister Linda washed the dishes and I dried and put them away, I would pass by the door and peer into the living room for another look at the piano. Finally I could resist no longer. I tiptoed into the parlor for a closer look. Before I knew it, I was sitting on the bench with one finger poised over the keys.

With precision, I tenderly hit a key. A second and a third followed until I'd played a perfect one-finger rendition of "Silent Night."

I'd barely been aware of my surroundings until, from the back of the house, I heard my mother's voice. "Who's playing the piano?"

Terrified because I knew I had disobeyed, I grabbed the dishtowel and dashed back to the kitchen. But not soon enough! Mom came around the corner behind me.

"Brenda, were you playing the piano just now?"

I nodded and started to cry.

Gently she touched my heaving shoulder. "Can you do it again for me?"

I started in surprise. *Aren't I in trouble for disobeying?* "Uh-huh."

She led me to the piano. I sat on the bench and played the carol again. With song after song, my mother would name the tune and I would play it with one finger. Soon the rest of the family gathered around to listen and began suggesting more songs for me to play.

Over the next few weeks Mom taught me how to add the appropriate chords to my one-note songs. My brothers and sisters made it a game of suggesting tunes to see if I could play them. When they ran out of familiar tunes, they made up songs, and I would reproduce them on the keyboard. Six months after playing my first note on the piano, I was playing for church and Sabbath School, sunshine bands, and prayer meetings. I still do today.

CHAPTER 7

Growing Up With Miracles

I believe in answered prayer. As terrible as my life was while I was married to Dave, I still knew that God delights in answering the prayers of His children. My childlike faith sustained me through the worst of times, I am sure. I remembered my father saying that whenever times were tough, "God is only testing our faith." I'd seen too many miracles while growing up in my parents' home, the unusual blending of people or events that couldn't be explained away by happenstance or chance.

I grew up hearing my mother tell of the day when Dad was driving down the busy Capital Avenue in Battle Creek, Michigan. Mom was holding my baby sister Cinda on her lap in the front seat. I was two years old and riding in the back seat of the car with my sister Linda. (Infant car seats and seat belts were merely a bright idea in the mind of an automobile engineer in Detroit back then.)

Mom turned around in time to catch me playing with the door handle. "Brenda, I've told you before: Don't play with the handle."

She'd barely turned around when our car crested the top of a steep incline and the door beside me swung open. I flew out of the car and hit the ground with a thud. Over and over, I tumbled down the hill.

Inside the car, Linda screamed. Dad stomped on the brakes. Before the car had come to a complete stop Mom had set Cinda down on the front seat and leaped from the car in a dead run. She reached me seconds before I rolled into the pathway of oncoming traffic. I was screaming in terror and indignation. Blood from a large gash on my chin gushed down the front of my blue-checkered coat and matching leggings. Mom scooped me up into her arms and rushed back to the car.

"Hurry! We've got to get her to the hospital!" Mom jumped into the back seat and slammed the car door while my father jammed his foot down on the accelerator.

"Is she all right?" He dared not turn around to see what condition I might be in.

"I-I-I don't know. Her chin is bleeding, but who knows what's going on inside."

The car squealed to a stop at the hospital emergency entrance. Clutching me to her chest, Mom leaped from the car and dashed into the building.

"Your daughter is one lucky little girl," the ER doctor commented as he stitched up my chin. "Other than the few cuts on her chin and a few scratches on her tummy, she's fine. Her heavy winter coat, leggings, and hat protected her from what could have been a very serious tragedy." For me, the lesson was learned. I never played with door handles again.

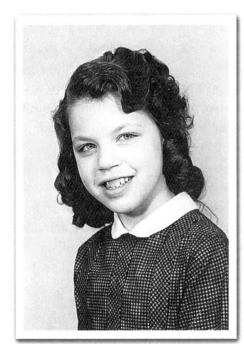

Brenda was baptized at the age of 10.

When I was ten we lived in Moline, Illinois. We girls and our younger brother Jim had to walk ten blocks to school every morning and return each evening the same way. Halfway to school a gigantic German shepherd would bark at us from behind the screened-in porch where it was tied.

Terrified that the dog would break free and chase us, we would check to be certain the dog was contained on the porch before running past the house at breakneck speed. One afternoon, as we passed the house on our way home, the dog began barking and crashing against the screen door. Terrified, Cinda froze and burst into tears.

"Run!" Linda yelled and grabbed Cinda's hand and tried to drag her, but Cinda wouldn't budge.

As the barking dog lunged against the porch door, the door jarred open, freeing the animal. Most children would have broken into a run. We didn't. Without saying a word to one another, we automatically knelt down in our family prayer circle, held hands, and Linda prayed.

"Dear Jesus, please help us. Close the dog's mouth so he can't hurt us." Her voice quivered as she prayed.

"Just like you did to those big lions for Daniel," Jimmy added.

Instinctively we opened our eyes to see where the dog was. Suddenly the animal stopped dead in its tracks, cocked its head to one side and gave us a curious glance. It then whipped around and, sounding as though it was in pain, yelped all the way back to the porch. The screen door slammed shut behind it.

We whispered a quick "Thank You, Jesus," rose to our feet, and ran all the way home, not because we were any longer afraid, but because we could hardly wait to tell our parents about how the angels shut the dog's mouth so that it couldn't hurt us.

Regardless of how lean their finances became, my parents insisted on providing Christian education for all of us children. When I was in fifth grade, we attended a two-room church school in Moline, Illinois. Mr. Hinkley was the principal and taught grades five through eight while his wife taught grades one through four.

For some reason money was tighter than usual. During one particular week, my father asked the family to pray extra prayers for him as he traveled door to door selling books. At school the next day, Linda and I decided to take turns going into the bathroom to pray for our father. We went several times that morning and again that afternoon. That night around the supper table Dad announced that he'd sold three books that day. Linda and I grinned at one another but said nothing.

A few minutes later, I asked, "What time was it when you sold all those books?"

My father thought for a moment. "Well, let's see. I sold the first one around nine-thirty in the morning, another one around one o'clock, and the last, it must have been around three. Why?"

I shrugged. "Just wondering."

As soon as the dishes were done and the kitchen straightened, Linda and I dashed into our bedroom and closed the door.

"Jesus answered our prayers," I said. I grabbed my sister's hands and jumped up and down. "At the same time we prayed, Dad sold a book."

Linda's eyes danced with excitement. "Let's pray harder tomorrow!"

By the end of a week of frequent trips to the restroom for us girls, Mr. Hinkley called Dad in for a parent-teacher consultation.

"I think there might be something wrong with your daughters," he began.

"Really? Why?"

"Well . . ." He was obviously uncomfortable discussing his suspicions. "Linda and Brenda run to the bathroom much too often for healthy girls. I'm wondering if they might have bladder infections. Perhaps you could talk with the girls. It would be less embarrassing coming from you, their father."

That evening after supper, my father came into our room and sat down on the end of our bed. "Girls, I need to talk to you about something." He sounded serious.

"Your principal says that the two of you are always running to the bathroom." He eyed us carefully. "If you don't have a bladder problem, I'm guessing you're in trouble!"

I shot a worried glance at Linda. Linda took a deep breath. "Dad, the truth is—"

I interrupted. "We are going into the bathroom to—"

"—pray for you throughout the day." Linda finished my sentence. "The other day we prayed for you at the exact times you sold books—"

"Jesus is answering our prayers!"

Tears filled our father's eyes. He stretched out his hands toward us. "Come over here, you half-pints." We ran into his arms to receive the biggest of hugs.

Pushing away from him for a moment, I asked, "But, Daddy, what do we do now that we can't go to the bathroom to pray anymore?"

He threw back his head and laughed. "You listen here—you girls keep going to the bathroom to pray, and I'll take care of your principal." And he did. Linda and I continued the practice throughout grade school.

My parents' prayers affected the choices I made as well. As I mentioned in an earlier chapter, I decided after my first year attending Wisconsin Academy, a Christian boarding school, that I wanted to make my own way. I was determined to attend Georgia-Cumberland Academy during my sophomore year. My parents lived near the academy in Columbus, Wisconsin, where my older sister Linda attended. I thought it would be fun to go to a school where people didn't know me as one of the Micheff girls. After much persuasion on my part, my parents relented.

Despite my parents' misgivings, my mother and I went shopping for my first store-bought dress—fourteen dollars at Kmart. I felt like a princess in it. I thought I would wear it forever, and I did, until it wore out. In a family where hand-me-downs were the norm, that feat alone was phenomenal.

My father drove me to the airport in Madison. I was wearing a new light-blue cotton dress that Mom had made for me. As I stood at the gate waiting to board my first jet plane, Dad took my hands in his and spoke the advice that would haunt me on my wedding day. "Bibby, I want you to know that you will make new friends at this school. Remember you will find just what you are looking for. You can choose friends who love Jesus or friends who don't. The choices you make will make a difference in your life forever."

Tears welled up in my eyes.

"Honey, I love you very much."

I nodded and sniffed.

"Please don't go anywhere you can't take Jesus with you."

I looked up into his face. Tears were streaming down his cheeks.

My father's words went with me throughout my high school experience. I was determined to make my father proud of me. Every time I was tempted by friends to sneak out of the dorm or to do something that was against the rules, I would see Daddy with tears running down his face, and I would walk away.

Brenda's senior photo from Georgia-Cumberland Academy

I loved Georgia-Cumberland Academy, and I had just completed the first semester of my senior year when I got a call. I was forced to make a heartbreaking decision. Mom and Dad phoned to say that they did not have the money to pay for my college entrance fees, and they felt terrible knowing how much I wanted to attend Southern Missionary College the next year. So they presented me with two options. I could finish out my senior year and graduate with my class at GCA. If I chose that option, I would not be able to go to college the next year. I would have to work for a year to earn my entrance fees and start college later. Or I could come back home second semester and live at home as a day student. I could get a job right away, earn the needed funds, and start college with my friends and classmates. This was an agonizing decision, as I felt bonded with my classmates in Georgia. After all, I had attended two and a half years there already. But the thought of not being with my friends in college was far worse. Thus, I made the decision to move home and attend Wisconsin Academy second semester. By this time my parents had moved to an eighty-acre farm about seven miles from the school.

You've never experienced a blizzard if you've never experienced a Midwestern blizzard. The winds howl around the corners of the house round the clock. Snow pelts the windows at a forty-five-degree angle. We could scratch our initials in the frost that formed on the inside of the house's double-paned storm windows.

After a horrendous snowstorm one night, we awakened to a world of sparkling sunlight and fresh snow. Cinda and I hated missing school for any reason. Being cooped up in the farmhouse all day with nothing to do when we could be at school with our friends didn't appeal to us.

At breakfast I broached the subject of going out. "Dad, it looks like the snow has stopped. Think the roads are clear enough that Cinda and I could drive to school this morning?"

"No! Absolutely not. I doubt the plows have had time to clear the state roads let alone the county ones."

"But, Daddy, I have a math quiz today. You know how important Mr. Rizzo's quizzes count into the final grade." I knew I was tapping on an important pressure point with my father—grades. When he paused to think, I shot a quick grin toward Cinda.

She nodded and smiled back.

I continued with my reasoning. "It will take Cinda and me ten minutes at the most to make the trip. I really do hate to miss that math test."

"Test? Now it's a math test?"

I gulped. "Er . . . well, test, quiz, I need every point I can get. Math is really hard for me."

Cinda picked up the cause. "Please, Daddy. I have an English paper due tomorrow. I need to spend time in the library to finish it."

"Please, please, please?" We both looked eagerly at him. When we glanced toward Mom for support, she shrugged as if to say, "Don't drag me into this. If your father says it's unsafe for you to go, it's unsafe."

Dad got up from the breakfast table, strode over to the kitchen window, and brushed aside the ruffled Priscilla curtain. "The storm clouds seem to have moved farther east, but the road hasn't been plowed yet. I'll tell you what. You girls don't have enough driving experience yet for these conditions, so I'll drive you to school."

"Great! I'll get my books!" I hopped up from the table and ran to my bedroom to retrieve my school supplies. Cinda did the same.

A few minutes later we'd piled into our green Volkswagen bug and were plowing through small snowdrifts toward the academy. We'd gone only a few miles when the sun disappeared behind heavy clouds and icy flakes began pelting our windshield. Dad hunched over the wheel, his attention focused on following a set of tire tracks in the center of the snow-covered roadway. Another mile and the tiny flakes had grown into a major snowstorm. Cinda and I looked at each other with worried expressions and silently began to pray. Accompanied by strong winds, the storm was fast becoming a blizzard.

The worse the storm grew, the better home seemed to me. "Maybe we should turn around," I said.

We held our breaths as the car sashayed on a slick of ice. Dad's whitened knuckles clutched the steering wheel. "I wouldn't dare. I can't tell where the pavement ends and the ditch begins." He glanced toward the odometer. "We're over half way there now."

I eyed the snowdrifts outside the car window. At some points they climbed half way up the telephone poles. Suddenly a huge gust of wind slammed into the side of our VW, sliding us out of control and into a snowbank with a thud. The impact loosened the snow on the bank and dumped it onto our car, almost obliterating us entirely.

"We've got to get out of here, girls." My father turned the door lever and pressed his shoulder against it. The door wouldn't budge. Next he rolled down his window and climbed out. Cinda and I followed.

The sparkling world of white had turned to a dull gray with wind whipping at the snow. Across a field we spotted a light that we assumed was outside a farmhouse, though we couldn't see the building. We shivered as the strong gusts and the cold temperature bit into our faces and through out heavy winter coats.

"Considering the windchill factor, it wouldn't take long to freeze out here." Dad pointed toward the light. "Run as fast as you can for the light!"

We stumbled through the drifts and across the snow-covered field, praying as we ran. Tears froze on my cheeks. My fingers grew so cold that I couldn't feel them.

"Come on, Cinda! Run!" I shouted as the wind forced my words back down my throat. I could hear my father running behind us. By the time we reached the fence we were out of breath and chilled through and through. We managed to scramble over the fence and onto the front porch of the big Midwestern farmhouse. The light had come from inside the house.

Cinda and I knocked on the door. No one answered. Desperately we pounded with our fists and shouted, "Help! Help! Please, dear Jesus, let someone open the door! Please, dear Jesus." Still no one came.

Behind us my father began searching for a brick or a piece of wood to break a window if necessary. "This should do it!" Dad picked up a chair off the porch and aimed it at the window in the door just as the door opened.

The farmer and his wife stared in surprise at the sight of a stranger poised to smash in their front-door window and two teenage girls shivering in the snow.

"What are you doing out in a blizzard like this?" The farmer opened the door farther.

"I was taking my daughters to school, and we slid into a snowbank." Dad set down the chair and extended his hand in greeting. "We knocked, and when no one answered, I—"

"Come in! Come in! Get out of that wind. You must be freezing. Martha," the farmer said to his wife, "these folks need a cup of your hot chocolate to warm up."

While Cinda and I drank the steaming brew, the two men discussed our problem.

The man stroked his chin thoughtfully. "My tractor should be able to pull a VW out of a ditch. Finish your hot chocolate, Mr. Micheff, while I bundle up. You girls stay here in the house with my wife while your father and I haul your car out of the snowbank."

Soon we said Goodbye to our new friends and were heading back home. When we pulled into the farmyard, Cinda and I bounded into the kitchen, eager to tell our mother about the answered prayer—and the farmer and his wife. In our gratitude and praise, Cinda's unfinished English paper and my missed math quiz were forgotten. But the lesson of God's protection would remain forever.

Interlude: A Single Mom in Texas

Life is a journey. My rocky road experience left me raw and wounded. Now, safe at home, I began to heal. I read in Scripture to find meaning and smiled as I came to Psalm 133:1:

Behold, how good and how pleasant it is
For brethren to dwell together in unity! (NKJV, italics supplied).

How very true, I thought. What a contrast this "interlude in Texas" is from the living hell I experienced in Kentucky.

I began to redefine my life, using Scripture as my guide. I asked, Who am I?

I kept reading to find an answer and began to insert my name into certain verses to make them personal. In Psalm 135, I read:

Praise the LORD, for the LORD is good;
Sing praises to His name, for it is pleasant.
For the LORD has chosen Brenda for Himself,
Brenda for His special treasure (NKJV, my own paraphrase).
I was hurting, but God was healing. Praise the Lord!

CHAPTER 8

Getting Back on Track

Living at home in Texas again, surrounded by those who loved me, I fell into a daily routine of caring for Becky and helping my mother with the housework. Healing didn't happen overnight for me. At first I couldn't leave the house without my daughter close by my side. My heart recoiled at the idea of trusting anyone outside my family. I wondered if I would ever feel normal again.

In time I knew I would one day be able to relax and almost enjoy myself even when Becky was out of my sight. In time I would be able to go to the grocery store without shaking in terror when I spotted a tall, muscular man who resembled Dave. In time I prayed that I wouldn't weep when I saw idyllic little families worshiping together in church. Everyone told me it would take time to heal, but I was impatient. I wanted to forget the past and get on with my new life.

With my year of nurse's training, I should have known healing would take time. If a broken leg takes time to heal, why wouldn't a broken spirit? Every morning I tried to remind myself that healing takes time and tender, loving care. My family could provide the TLC, but only God held the hourglass of time.

My nights were the worst. While the house was still, I would lie in bed and listen to Becky as she made those precious baby sounds in her sleep. I would thank God for her all over again. I would stare at the patterns of light and darkness dancing on the ceiling and wish I could somehow avoid closing my eyes.

Eventually, despite my resistance, I would drift into a restless slumber and the nightmares would return. At times in my dreams I'd be driving my car along the interstate with Becky asleep on the seat beside me and I'd see the flashing light of a police car and hear the siren warning me to pull over. My heart would pound as a uniformed patrolman swaggered to my car, thrust his beefy fist through the car's open window, and grabbed me by the throat. Or I'd be stumbling through a field with Dave firing his gun at me. I could hear the explosions; I could feel the bullets zinging past my body. Try as I might, like an actor filmed in slow motion, I couldn't escape.

Other times I would find myself in a fetal position on the floor, with my ex-husband looming over me, kicking me with his heavy boot. By the time I regained consciousness, I would be covered with sweat, sobbing and crying in fear.

The nightmares continued until one night when I awakened myself with a blood-curdling scream. I couldn't stop screaming and shaking. The bedroom door flew open and my parents rushed into the room.

While my father checked the windows for intruders, my mother wrapped me in her arms. "Brenda! Are you all right?"

"No! He was here again, in my dreams! It was all so real!"

My father sat down beside me and put his arms around both of us. I buried my face in his chest. I could feel his heart pounding hard against my face. My nightmares were taking a toll on my parents as well.

"Oh, Daddy, will these nightmares ever stop?"

"I don't know if they're from the devil or from fear lingering in your subconscious. But it's time we ask the Lord to tear down this evil stronghold!" My father straightened, took one of my mother's hands and one of mine in his, bowed his head and began to pray. "Heavenly Father, 'perfect love, casts out fear'—Your perfect love. I know that You love my precious daughter even more than I do. And Your love can see how these horrid nightmares are destroying the peace that You promised to deliver to her through the fruit of the Spirit."

My breath continued to come in short, helpless gasps. It had been so long since I'd felt peace of any kind. Was it really possible to experience the peace of my childhood once again?

"Her innermost being, the one You saw even before she was formed in her mother's womb has been wounded badly, Lord. You are the One who can restore health and peace to her mind, her body, and her spirit. You are our Healer!" I could hear the tears in his voice and the pain in his heart. "As Your faithful children, we claim on her behalf the promises You made throughout Your Word, the promise of divine healing."

The confidence in my father's voice soothed me as it had done so often when I was a child. But I wasn't a child any longer. I was a woman who'd been battered, beaten, and almost destroyed. Would prayer have the power to heal my inner wounds as it had the scrapes and bruises I'd experienced as a little child?

The war in my mind continued. So did my father's prayer.

"We claim the authority You gave us on Calvary when You defeated the evil one. Through You, we are more than conquerors! And we come against the strongholds of Satan tonight! Just as Moses came before Pharaoh and cried, 'Let My people go!' so I stand before Lucifer and all the defeated forces of evil, and demand in Your Son's holy name, 'Let my daughter go!' End these nightmares here and now! Surround her with heavenly angels. Place a hedge of peace about her."

I don't remember how long we prayed, but by the time they kissed me good night and my mother tucked the blankets under my chin, my heart was filled with peace and hope. The nightmares never returned.

As God's restorative balm of love and time began to soothe my painful memories, I knew that it was time to move forward with my life. I had a baby to support. My parents couldn't afford to support me forever. At dinner each evening I talked about getting a job. One evening I considered waitressing at a local diner, or attending night school to become a beautician.

My parents patiently listened as I floated each idea past them. Finally Mom asked, "Brenda, if you could do anything in the world, what would you really like to do?"

"Well, as you know, I always dreamed of becoming a nurse, but I can't see—"

"Nonsense!" My father clicked his tongue in objection. "What's stopping you? Get back into nursing and make something of yourself!"

"But, Dad, I have a daughter to raise, and I can't—"

"Can't? If you really want to, you can."

"You know that Daddy and I will help you in any way we can. We are more than willing to care for Becky while you go back to school," my mother added enthusiastically.

Dad leaned forward, his mind shifting into full gear. "As you know, Cinda begins her one-year training to become a licensed practical nurse next month. If you enrolled in the program with her you would be an LPN in a year. If you wanted to get your RN, you could do that later."

A plan was taking shape. Maybe, just maybe, I could complete my training and accomplish something after all. "I-I-I'll call tomorrow and see if they have any openings."

That night I could hardly sleep. All the dreams that had been trampled under Dave's heavy boot sprang back to life. New possibilities teased my imagination.

The next morning I called the school and learned that registration for the program was closed until the following year. *Maybe if I went in and presented my case, surely an exception could be made,* I thought. Mom watched Becky while I drove to the school to meet with the registrar.

"I am sorry." The registrar's lips tightened into a pucker. "The class is full, and registration is closed for this year."

"And there's no possible exception that can be made?" I was desperate.

"Absolutely not. Policy is policy, you know. You will have to wait to apply until we open the registration for next year's class." Her words and demeanor left no room for compromise. Whether I liked it or not, I would have to wait a year. What would I do in the meantime?

Knowing my tears were about to flow—at that point in my life I cried at the drop of a handkerchief—I fled the office for the sanctuary of my car. Once inside I pounded the steering wheel in frustration. "Why, Lord? Why must everything in my life be so difficult?" I tried to stop the tears long enough to drive home safely. But once I was safe in the arms of my family, a dam inside of me burst. I threw myself on my bed and cried. Between sobs I told my parents what had happened. "Doesn't God want me to get my life back on track?"

"Honey, of course He does. Remember the promise in Jeremiah, chapter 29, verse 11? ' "For I know the plans I have for you," declares the LORD, "plans to prosper you and not to harm you, plans to give you hope and a future" ' (NIV). That's His promise, not mine. He loves you so much, more than Mama and I do, if such a thing is possible. He holds the answer for you." My father took my hand in his and began to pray for God to reveal His plan for me. "If nursing isn't in Brenda's immediate future, direct her in the way You would have her go. In the meantime, fill her with Your love and Your peace."

After they left the room, I curled into a tight little ball and slept. I awakened several hours later. Realizing it was near dinnertime, I hurried out to the kitchen to help Mom prepare our meal. I'd finished setting the table when Dad burst through the kitchen door, his face wreathed with smiles. "God has answered our prayers! Bibby, God has a plan for your life, and He demonstrated it today!"

My breath caught in my throat. "What? How?"

"You will never believe it. I took the car to the dealer to have it worked on." His grin widened. "You'll never guess who I met in the waiting area. I struck up a conversation with the man sitting next to me."

That was nothing unusual. My dad talked with everyone he met.

"In the course of our conversation, I told him about you and Dave, and your precious baby girl. I told him how you were trying to get your life back together and had tried to get into the LPN program but the class was closed, and how discouraged you were."

By then I was cringing with embarrassment. I wasn't sure I wanted the entire world to know of my humiliating situation. And yet my heart was thumping with excitement.

"At the end of my story, the man turned to me and said, 'I am the president of the school. You bring your daughter to see me in the morning. I will make sure she gets into that class.' "

"A-i-i-ah!" I screamed, cried, and danced in circles.

"See? I told you that God had a plan for you." Dad grabbed my hand and my mom's hand. We knelt on the kitchen floor and thanked God for the incredible answer to our prayer.

The next morning when I arrived at the school all the paperwork had been cleared, and I was enrolled in the nursing program.

Going to school with Cinda was the best therapy for me. She is a loving, generous person with a wild and crazy sense of humor. It is hard to feel sorry for yourself when she's around making you laugh all the time. Immediately distinguishing herself as the class clown, she made even the most disgusting tasks fun.

One day while working on the hospital floor, I watched as Cinda kept coming out of a patient's room, burying her nose in her shoulder and then disappearing back inside her patient's room.

After about the fourth or fifth trip, I asked her, "What in the world are you doing?"

Cinda giggled. "I'll let you in on a little secret. My patient has a terrible case of diarrhea. While I'm cleaning it up, the smell almost gags me. To keep from being sick myself, I sprayed perfume on my shoulders. Whenever the odors get to me, I run from the room, sniff the perfume to clear my senses, and return to do whatever I need to do."

"You've got to be kidding!" I threw back my head and laughed.

"Hey, believe it or not, it works."

At the end of the year, Cinda and I graduated with straight A's—a miracle in itself considering what an emotional wreck I was. Cinda went to work in the intensive care unit at Berrien Springs General Hospital in Michigan. Saying goodbye hurt after we'd had such a special year together. I was hired on at the training hospital in Texas as a scrub nurse in the surgery department. I loved it.

Six months into the nursing program, I met James, a naval flight surgeon and a captain in the United States Navy. I knew his parents, Ola and Oscar, before I met him. They were members in one of my father's churches. Everyone called Ola "Grammy," and I did too. On Sabbath afternoons when Oscar didn't feel well enough to attend church, I would drive out to their place to play the piano and sing for them. Their love for Jesus was beautiful. They dreamed of one day being together as a family in heaven.

Oscar, a specialist in reflexology, taught me how to give a foot massage like I'd never had before and how to relieve a headache by pressing on various pressure points in the feet. In the process of teaching me these useful and fascinating skills, the couple told me about their son, James. He was a medical doctor and had graduated from the Loma Linda University School of Medicine in southern California. He had joined the navy right out of medical school. Not only was he a captain in the United States Navy but he also had degrees in aerospace medicine, emergency medicine, and acceleration physiology, and extensive training in psychology.

"My James is single," Grammy said. "He's never been married." She showed me photos of him. "You two are perfect for each other." Oscar teased me that one day I would be his daughter-in-law.

Then, as Oscar's health deteriorated, he was hospitalized in the facility where I was a nursing student. When I was off duty I would stay with Oscar, many times all night, to give Grammy a break. I would look in on him while I was on duty. I asked the nurses on the floor to treat him with extra special care because he was a very special man.

I met James when Oscar became sick to the point of death. Taking a leave of absence from the navy, he came home to spend time with his dad. James and I became acquainted during the long nights of caring for his dad. While Oscar slept much of the time, I would come into his room every two hours to turn him, fluff his pillows, and give him sips of water.

One night James and I were chatting while I administered Oscar's pain medication. "And you know, James—"

"Call me Jim."

"Jim? But everyone calls you James."

He shrugged and sent me a sly little grin. "I know. That's why I'd like it if you called me Jim instead."

"All right, Jim," I replied, smiling back.

Jim had a way of encouraging me to talk about my pain with him, to share the memories I'd tried to bury inside. Sometimes it was so difficult I would find myself sobbing. I'd never told anyone what I'd been through, not even Linda. A part of me still insisted on taking the blame for all that had happened. And because I thought it was my fault, I was embarrassed to let my family know just how bad things really were.

Through one memory after another, he would coax the terrible remembrance from me. "Have you dealt with this?" he would ask. He would say, "You realize that was not your fault," or "You need to put that on the shelf and never take it down again." Again and again he would say, "Don't go there. You did nothing wrong." To this day the most painful of those memories have "stayed on the shelf." Some things were so horrible that Jim insisted I never think about them again. He taught me that even if something triggered a bad memory that I should immediately push it from my mind. To this day, I have never allowed myself to revisit those darkest memories, not even for this book. I realize that it is only by God's amazing grace that this is even possible.

Thanks to Jim's quiet, gentle probing, my heart began to heal over the months that followed. I began smiling real smiles, not the plastic ones that I flashed when I thought it was expected of me; not the ones that I hid behind. I felt alive again, truly alive! If I'd had to pay a psychologist for all the hours of therapy Jim gave freely, I could not have afforded it. But God used this man, through His power, to make me whole again. A new Brenda emerged—not the naïve girl I'd been two years before, but a more self-confident woman, although a little less trusting, especially when it came to men.

I determined that no man would ever hit me again. No man would ever again take control of my mind. I vowed that Jesus, and Jesus alone, would control my life. I claimed the promise, "He giveth power to the faint; and to them that have no might he increaseth strength" (Isaiah 40:29, KJV).

What I didn't count on was for our friendship to move to a more personal level. Before either of us knew what had happened, we were deeply in love with one another. Jim had healed my heart and I loved him for that, but more importantly, I loved him for the incredible person he was on the inside. He was probably the most intelligent man I'd ever met. I was happy to be in love with such a kind, gentle man. And I was in awe that he would be the slightest bit interested in me. One night I told him so.

He laughed. "Are you kidding? I fell in love with you the first night I saw you caring for my dad. Right then and there, you completely stole my heart."

I loved our long talks together. He shared his experiences working his way through medical school selling religious books. He was called a literature evangelist. I could relate to that because my father had done the same thing for a living during my childhood years. Jim and I would have spiritual discussions that could last all through dinner. He also loved astronomy and spent a great deal of time teaching me about the stars. His favorite constellation was Orion, which was mine too.

The time came when Oscar died. My father spoke at his funeral, and I played the organ. Together Grammy, Jim, his brothers and sisters, and I grieved over our loss. With his father gone, Jim had to return to the USS *Midway,* where he was senior medical officer. I cried and cried when he left. I'd come to love and depend on him so much.

After he left, Becky and I spent a lot of time with Grammy, trying to ease her loneliness. She had a back bedroom with two double beds. She'd sleep in one while Becky and I slept in the other. Long after Becky fell asleep, Grammy and I would talk, sometimes into the wee hours of the morning. She'd share stories about her James when he was a child, and I'd tell her about some of the special moments my Jim and I had shared together. Sometimes we'd laugh so hard we'd almost awaken Becky.

Jim and I exchanged letters daily. Every evening before going to bed I would write a long letter telling him in great detail about my day. While much of my news was trivial I would sometimes ask his advice on helping a particular patient. I loved sharing my life with someone who was truly interested in me.

At Jim's encouragement, I returned to college to complete my RN degree. With him being gone at sea for much of the time, I had lots of time to study. My folks arranged to rent a little one-bedroom house closer to the college for Becky and me. While taking classes, I worked at a local hospital to cover our other living expenses. The next few months were spent juggling work, school, and motherhood. It was a busy time, but a happy time.

CHAPTER 9

Romance and Regrets

The love songs, the flowers, the tender moments I'd missed with Dave—Jim romanced me with all of them in style. We did a lot of "first time" things together. My growing up as a preacher's kid in a family of five didn't leave much money for firsts. First times were very important to Jim. He loved giving me as many of those special moments as possible. And that's why being with Jim was always an adventure.

I had not been to many restaurants in my life. He loved to take me to an exotic restaurant and order for me, and then watch my reaction when I tasted a new and different dish.

Another "first" with Jim was backpacking in California. Having to carry my own pack, I soon learned what to take along and what to leave behind. As nice as a meal of freshly scrambled eggs, tomato soup from a can, and peanut butter pancakes might be on the trail, a lighter pack was so much better.

We'd been dating for three glorious years. Either he'd come home on leave or I would travel to see him. Whenever I did so, Becky would stay with my parents or with Grammy.

The first time he asked me to marry him we'd gone camping at Yosemite National Park. After a brisk hike to the top of El Capitan, we found a secluded spot with an excellent view of Bridal Veil Falls, where we could eat our lunch. We'd finished eating and I was packing up the leftovers when he stood up and put his arms around me with my back to his chest. "Look," he whispered in my ear.

A pristine sunlight bathed the valley below. From our vantage point we could have been the first pioneers to stumble onto the exquisite beauty of the place. Silently we stood in awe for several moments. I could sense that he was filled with emotion. I detected something different about him. Giving me an extra squeeze, he turned me around to face him.

"Brenda, meeting you is the most important thing that has happened to me in my life. Before I met you there was such an aching in my heart and emptiness in my life such as I can't begin to describe.

"You have filled my heart with so much love that if I died today, I would die a happy man. I can't imagine my life without you. Without you, there *is* no me!" His voice broke with emotion. "I want to wake up every morning with you beside me and I want to kiss you good night every night. I want to grow old with you." He swallowed hard and continued. "Brenda, what I'm trying to say is that I love you with all my heart and I am asking you to marry me."

I was stunned. This was not what I'd expected. Yes, we had talked about future plans and always we were together in those plans, but he had not spoken of marriage. He hadn't even hinted of it!

My mind was spinning so fast I could hardly breathe. I gazed inquiringly into his eyes. A small tear spilled down his cheek. I reached up to wipe it away. More than anything in the world, I wanted to scream with delight, "Yes! I will marry you!" But there had been no mention of Becky. Not one word. I didn't want to mention her for fear that he would just go through the motions of loving her for my sake. I wanted more for Becky. I wanted her to have a father who absolutely adored her for the delightful child she was—not just because she was my daughter.

I decided Jim needed more time to get to know her. Becky was so precious. I just knew he would learn to love her as I did if they were just given the chance to spend more time together.

Continuing to search his face, I took a deep breath before giving him my reply. "Jim, I love you desperately—more than I ever thought possible. I can't imagine my life without you but . . ." A veil of disappointment fell over his eyes. "But I'm not ready to make a permanent commitment. I-I-I need more time. Please give me more time?"

He gathered me into his arms and held me tight. I sensed he was disappointed and hurt. I cried for having caused him pain.

He stroked my hair tenderly. "Now there's nothing to cry about, darling. I'm not going anywhere. If you need more time, we will wait. I would wait for you forever!" He tilted my chin up to meet his lips and kissed me.

I am sure he thought my hesitancy was due to my horrific first marriage. It wasn't. I'd been waiting to see a bond of love develop between him and Becky, not one encouraged by me. I wanted it to come naturally. Becky and I came as a "package deal." I knew that one word from me and he would move heaven and earth to accede to my wishes, but that wouldn't have been a natural affection.

In my prayers I would lift Jim and Becky up to the Father. "I don't understand it, Lord. She is such a sweet and adorable child. Why aren't they bonding after all this time? I love them both so much. Please help me to know Your will."

Becky was almost four years old and beautiful inside and out. She was the joy of my life. We went everywhere together except when I left her behind when visiting Jim. And of course, I thought she had to be the smartest little girl in the world. While I studied for my nursing exams, she studied with me. As a result, she learned the medical names for most of the bones and muscles in her body.

I remember getting a call from her preschool teacher. The woman wanted to talk with me about Becky when I picked her up from school the next afternoon. I was stunned when she told me, "Yesterday, Becky came to me saying one of her classmates had knocked her down and had made her cry. She said, 'I need a Kleenex tissue because I have rhinorrhea, and look at my leg! Now I'll have ecchymosis!'"

The teacher continued. "When she has to go to the bathroom she tells me that she must void or defecate. What child talks like this? I don't even know what she's talking about."

Relieved that nothing bad had happened, I laughed out loud. "As you know, Becky is a fast learner, and she loves having me read to her. So, while I've been studying for my finals, I've been reading my medical books to her."

While most little girls love to play house, Becky loved to play church. With her "Papa" pastoring four churches and my playing for most of the services, she spent more time in church than most children her age. On

Sabbath afternoons we would go on "sunshine bands" to nursing homes. During the week we also attended prayer meetings.

Becky loved riding up front, standing in the middle next to Papa (before the days of car seats in vehicles). She would say, "Papa, let's play church," and then ask my father to preach. She would interrupt in the middle of his "sermon" and announce, "Now it's Nana's turn to have special music."

While Jim was very good to her, he never tried to draw her to him. And until I saw the appropriate love developing between the two, I knew that I could not and would not marry him.

During the year that followed, he repeatedly asked his question, and I repeatedly deferred my answer. When I graduated with my RN degree, he was there to celebrate with me. Again I watched for signs of a growing love between the two most important people in my life. Again I saw none.

When he came back from sea duty and was assigned to the ER at the base hospital in Key West, Florida, we celebrated being able to see one another more often. In the weeks that followed his reassignment, letters, phone calls, and airplanes flew between Florida and Texas. I loved my weekends with him, especially walking along the beach together and watching the sun set over the ocean.

One night we'd finished dinner at a quaint little restaurant near the beach. The sun's vivid colors of yellow, purple, red, and pink on the water seemed to go on forever. We strolled along arm in arm until we came to a bench where we sat down to absorb the incredible light show. We'd talked nonstop during dinner, but now a comfortable silence lingered between us.

Brenda with her parents and nephew Jimmy, after her graduation as a registered nurse.

"I've been thinking about whether or not to re-enlist, and I wanted to see what you thought. I've been thinking about leaving the navy and setting up private practice near my family farm in Breckenridge. I know it's a small town, but I'm sure they could use medical help. You could be my nurse and run the office. What would you think of that?"

I nodded my head enthusiastically, already forming visions in my mind. At the time I was living with my folks in Mineral, Texas, a half-hour away. He continued describing his plan for building a house for us on the farm. Suddenly he turned toward me. "Brenda, let's get married! You could search the world over and not find another man who would love you more than I do. I need you in my life every day! I want to tell everyone that you're my wife! Please say yes."

His heart was in his eyes as he kissed me first on both cheeks and then on the lips. "Do you want me to get down on one knee? Hey, I'll do better than that; I'll get down on both knees!" He moved to do so, but I held him back.

"Do I hear a 'but' coming?"

I nodded my head. "Honey, please let's not talk about it tonight. It's such a beautiful night, I just want to feel your arms around me and enjoy every second of being with you." Again I had hurt him. I could see it in his eyes. He put his arms around me and gave me a hug.

"All right, beautiful. But soon we have to talk about it. We need to make plans for our lives, and *you* are my life!"

I glanced away, as my heart was breaking too. Again there'd been no mention of Becky. We'd been together almost four years now, and still I saw no bond forming between them. *How long can this go on?* I wondered.

With all the trips I was making to Florida it seemed sensible for me to find a place so that I could be nearer to him. As usual, I prayed about this momentous decision. "I don't want to run ahead of You, Lord. Over the last four years, I've allowed You to guide each step in this relationship. If I'm not supposed to rent a place in Key West, I need to know."

The next time I visited, Jim met me, as usual, with a flourish of affection and love. That evening we went to eat at a Cuban restaurant, which was fast becoming a favorite of mine. Moments after we were seated, the waiter took our orders. I loved the Cuban black beans and salsa. While we waited for our food to arrive, Jim took my hand in his and gently caressed my fingertips with his lips.

"Brenda, there's something we need to discuss."

The somber tone in his voice set off warning bells in my mind. On his face I could see signs of internal stress.

"You know how you talked on the phone with Becky before we left the house? And then I spoke with her?"

"Yes?"

"Well, Becky said something that has really upset me."

I gulped in surprise. Becky? My Becky? Whatever could she have said that would upset him so?

"Becky ended our conversation with 'Good night, Daddy.' " He paused for a moment. I was speechless. A deadly silence engulfed us both for several seconds. Finally he added, "Brenda, I don't want Becky to call me Daddy because I am not her father."

If a tropical hurricane had swept through the restaurant it wouldn't have been more devastating. I found it difficult to breathe. Though I'd lost my appetite, I picked at the food placed before me. We ate our dinner in silence, a rarity for us. We both sensed something was terribly wrong.

That night I wrestled with myself. God had made it clear to me: I was not to marry Jim. There was no doubt in my mind. But my heart was breaking. Becky deserved a daddy who would love and adore her and not just a male presence who would tolerate her for her mother's sake.

I knew what I must do. The next morning I called my sister Linda and told her all that had happened. "Just come up and stay with me for a while," she pleaded. "The apartment over our house is empty, and you and Becky can stay there as long as you like."

I quickly packed what few clothes I had with me, booked a flight to Michigan, and headed for the airport. I left behind all the gifts Jim had given me. I didn't want him to think for one moment that I had dated him because I cared only for material things and not for him.

Before leaving I spent four hours composing a letter to Jim, saying I loved him deeply but that it was over between us. I told him I couldn't possibly plan a life with someone who couldn't love my daughter as much as she deserved to be loved. I thanked him for everything he'd done for me, but mostly for loving me. Our memories would be with me forever. I said I would explain more later. I quickly put the letter in the mailbox before I changed my mind. Then I climbed into the cab for the ride to the airport. As I glanced back and remembered the good times we had enjoyed in Key West, I wept. I knew I was taking the coward's way out, but I knew that the moment he looked in my eyes, I would be powerless to leave him.

Numb with grief, I made my way onto the small commuter plane, found my seat by the window, and buckled up. All the good times I'd had with Jim flashed through my mind—the exotic dishes we'd eaten at out-of-the-way restaurants, the endless hours talking, the hikes, the endless list of "firsts." What would my parents think? What would Grammy think? Everyone had seen such promise in our relationship. I dissolved in a torrent of tears. I was crying so hard I barely noticed the man who sat down beside me.

"Ma'am? Is there something I can do to help?" he drawled.

I shook my head and riffled through my purse, desperately searching for a tissue.

"Here." He held out a man-sized handkerchief for me to use. I snatched it from his hand and buried my face in the soft white cotton. I was still crying too hard to talk. "My name's Steve."

I glanced at him and nodded. Steve, a tall man, was having a difficult time folding up his long legs in the plane's narrow leg space. He saw my glance and chuckled. "They're building these seats closer and closer together. I guess they think everyone has short legs."

I sniffled into his handkerchief again.

"I usually fly my own jet to Florida, but it's grounded with mechanical problems and I had to go commercial. It stinks!"

Again I nodded as if I understood or cared about what he was saying. I'd never ridden on a private jet, though Jim had taken me on a private plane once. *I wonder if they're the same. Jim . . .* A new bout of tears poured from my eyes.

By now the plane had taxied down the runway and was preparing for takeoff. When I lowered the handkerchief for a moment, Steve tipped his head as if to peek up into my face.

"Who would make a beautiful girl like you cry? Do you want to talk about it? Some say I'm a good listener."

I eyed him suspiciously for an instant. Maybe it would help to talk to someone. What harm would it be to tell a perfect stranger? By the time we landed in Miami, where Steve owned a large welding company, I hadn't even gotten to the part about why I had to leave. When the wheels touched down on the runway, I was still crying.

"I can't let you travel to Michigan all by yourself like this! I'm going with you to Michigan. I want to make sure you get there all right."

"Oh, no! Please don't do that! I'll be fine." I was appalled at his suggestion. "Thank you, but no!" Although I was grateful for his listening ear, I wanted no part of a relationship with him or any other man for that matter. *No,* I thought, *better to say goodbye and leave it at that!*

I walked away and found my connecting flight. As I waited to board the aircraft, I spotted a very tall, muscular, sandy-haired man ambling toward the ticket counter. *No! It couldn't be!* But it was. *Wow! He's really tall!* Crossing the waiting area, Steve held up two tickets. "Come on, little lady. We're riding first class. And they're boarding us now."

"But, I . . ." I was speechless.

"I believe you have the rest of a story to tell me. I couldn't leave without hearing the ending." *Oh, that's just great! Now what am I supposed to do? But he did seem nice enough and a perfect gentleman.* Right then and there I should have thanked him for his kindness but firmly insisted on flying by myself. Once again, I didn't listen to that still, small voice.

I'd never met anyone quite like Steve. On the plane, he urged me to continue my sad tale of woe. By the time we landed, my tears had abated and I'd stopped talking long enough to learn that he was single, never been married, loved to travel, had too much money to spend and wrestled alligators for sport. A couple of times a year he would fly to Key West to compete for the alligator wrestling title. I'd never heard of such a thing.

At the airport in Michigan, Steve and I parted before I greeted my sister. He said he was going to catch the next flight back to Miami. I never expected to see or hear from him again, as I had been very careful not to give out any contact information.

Linda and I drove to her home in Grayling, Michigan. I had barely set my suitcases down when the phone rang. Linda answered it, and, covering the mouthpiece with her hand, she whispered to me, "It's Jim!"

"Tell him I can't talk with him yet!" I whispered back. I knew at the very sound of his voice all my resolve would disappear and I would be on the first flight to Florida.

I missed him terribly, but whenever I had a weak moment and headed for the phone to call him, I would think of Becky and how she deserved a father who would love her. I spent many nights crying until I thought my heart would break. Jim kept calling, and I kept refusing his calls.

The next weekend, Steve showed up at my sister Linda's place unannounced. I was shocked to see him again. *How did he find me?* I made certain he knew that he couldn't pop into my life without warning whenever he felt like it. Then I demanded to know how he had found me. He just laughed and said it was amazing what a little money could do. "I made one phone call to a detective, and, well, here I am!"

Now I was not only angry but also worried. Even though he seemed like a nice enough person, he was still a complete stranger and certainly not a Christian. I would have never considered dating him—I had learned my lesson! I was repulsed by the way this man kept intruding into my life when I thought I had made it clear I wasn't interested. *Oh, what have I done? Why did I spill my guts to him, much less let him fly with me! He must have thought I was interested in him.*

"The last thing I want right now is to get into another relationship. You of all people should know that, after listening to me pour out my heart to you for several hours." With a wounded puppy look in his eyes, he agreed to respect my privacy. I asked him not to contact me again and made sure he understood that there was no future for us.

The next day a truck pulled up in front of Linda's house with a delivery for me. I assured the driver that I hadn't ordered anything.

He showed me a large package. "Is that your name?"

"Yes, but I didn't order anything."

"Ma'am, I'm just paid to make the deliveries. You don't owe me anything. It's all paid for." He showed me the name on the package. It was from Steve.

Throwing my hands into the air, I insisted that whatever it was should be sent back. But the driver and his assistant acted as though they had not heard me and continued to carry several boxes from the truck and set them on the ground in front of Linda's place. Again I told them to put it back on the truck. Whatever was in those boxes, I did not want. The men ignored me, got in their truck, and drove away. When I opened the boxes I gasped in surprise. It was a beautiful stereo system, cabinet and all, obviously very expensive.

I called the delivery company to have them pick up the stereo. They told me that if I wanted to return it I would have to pay the shipping fees, which would have been more than two hundred dollars. That wasn't even a possibility for me! I had no money, and I was forced to admit defeat. I told my sister Linda that I didn't even want the stereo in my house. She said she didn't own a stereo, so I gladly gave it to her. I wanted nothing more to do with Steve or his gifts.

CHAPTER 10

Strangers in Strange Places

I had hoped that my last conversation with Steve would end his interest in me, but I was not going to get out of this mess so easily. He didn't stop calling, visiting, or sending elaborate gifts. Exasperated, I finally went to see the local police. Unfortunately, I could do nothing because he had not broken any laws. The next time he called, I demanded that he leave me alone and told him that I never wanted to hear from him again. I thought I'd sufficiently dampened his ardor until a few days later when I went to town to run a few errands. During the course of my shopping, I had the distinct impression that I was being followed. I scolded myself. *You're just being paranoid!*

I thought about and prayed about my suspicions all night. The next morning I went shopping again. I had to prove or disprove my concern. Sure enough, as I drove in a serpentine route through the small Midwestern town, a nondescript black car followed me. In the mall's store windows, I caught the image of a stranger ducking out of sight whenever I turned to look. Furious, I stormed home and called Steve.

"Are you having me followed?" At first he denied it but soon rescinded the denial.

"Yes . . . I wasn't doing it to frighten you. I'm afraid for you. I'm doing it for your protection."

"Well, call him off right now!"

"But I love you and I want to marry you! Don't you understand?"

"You don't even know me. I don't love you, and I don't want to marry you. For that matter I don't ever want to see you again! No more gifts! No more calls! And call off your hounds!"

Three months passed. My sister Linda's husband was working as the assistant camp director of Camp Au Sable, an Adventist youth camp in Michigan, and Linda was the cook. Linda had also offered to help with Becky while I got a job in a local hospital. It was a great solution for Becky. If I couldn't be with her all the time, at least she could be with family members. How could I trust my precious gift from God with a baby-sitter?

The time came for me to take my nursing state board exams, and I would have to take them in Texas, the state in which I had taken my training. Mom and Dad were now living in Alma, Michigan, only two hours away from my sister's place. They had generously agreed to take care of Becky for me while I took my boards. I packed our suitcases, trying to think of everything we would need over the next two weeks.

I looked at the suitcase stuffed with Becky's and my clothing and shook my head. *Where do all these things come from? How can a five-year-old need so much for such a short time?* With great effort I closed the case, and right then the telephone rang. I hesitated for a moment. *Is this a call I want to accept or not?* Thinking it might be Linda wanting me to take something home to Mom, I answered it. I wasn't prepared for the familiar voice on the other end of the telephone. It was Jim. My mouth went dry. I couldn't speak.

"Don't hang up, Brenda. Please don't hang up. You've got to hear me out. You owe me that much. You can't just throw away four years like they never happened."

Feeling guilty for the abrupt way I broke off our relationship, I wavered. With his warm, loving voice, all the memories and the loneliness I'd felt since we parted began to wash over me. Tears welled up in my eyes.

"Your letter didn't explain everything. I love you very much. Please, if after we talk you still choose to walk away, I'll let you go."

Through my tears I told him I was on my way to Texas to take my state boards. "I'll be in Dallas tomorrow. We can talk there." Perhaps on neutral soil I would be better able to maintain my emotional balance. After we hung up, however, I began to question the wisdom of seeing Jim. "Lord, let me know whether or not we should meet. Please give me some kind of a sign."

My head was in turmoil as Becky and I drove to my folks' place. I arrived early. This allowed Becky time to play with her friend Susie, a neighbor girl. I didn't mention anything about Jim's phone call or my decision to see him while I was in Dallas. That night when I put Becky to bed, Dad came into my daughter's room to tuck her in. Her bedtime prayer brought tears to my eyes.

"Dear Jesus, this is Becky. I just wanted to ask if I could have a daddy like Susie has. I promise that if You will give me a daddy, I will be a good girl and I'll do everything Mama tells me. Jesus, I really need a daddy to play with me. Please Jesus, please send me a daddy. Amen."

After kissing her and tucking her into bed, my father and I stepped out into the hallway. I discovered I wasn't the only one with tears in my eyes. Dad put his arm around me and whispered, "Bibby, let's go to my office. I understand how lonely you are; so does God. Your mom and I are so proud of you and the way you are bringing up your daughter in the ways of God. But I believe God has someone special for you and Becky." For two hours Dad and I claimed promises from the Word. And through our tears we pleaded with God to bring a Christian husband into my life, one who would be a loving father for Becky. That night, on our knees before the Lord, I could never have imagined what God had in store for Becky and for me.

The next morning Dad loaded my luggage into his car while I kissed Becky goodbye. "Now you be a good girl for Nana," I reminded her. "I'll see you in two weeks."

"I will, Mommy." Her bright brown eyes flashed with sincerity. "And I'll pray for you as you take your big test."

"Oh, thank you, sweetie. That means so much to me." Outside my father honked the horn, reminding me that we had to hurry. "Gotta go." I kissed her cheek. "Love you! Two and two!" "Two and two" was our pet goodbye, meaning "Two and two, you and me forever."

"Love you too, Mommy."

I turned toward my mother. "Thanks, Mom. I really appreciate—"

"Go! Go! You don't want to miss your flight."

I bounded out the back door. When I reached the driveway, I turned and waved to the two most beautiful women in my life.

On the way to the airport, Dad and I talked about Becky's prayer. He glanced over toward me as he swung the car onto the freeway. "I just know God is going to answer your prayer for a good Christian husband for you and a father for Becky. Soon, in fact."

I smiled. "You know, Dad, after our prayers last night, God gave me an incredible peace about this. He has someone, and I don't think it's Jim." In my heart I believed that meeting Jim in Dallas was to bring closure for both of us. And he was right; I did owe him that much. But with the butterfly activity in my stomach, I knew I was getting anxious over seeing him again.

After I checked in at the ticket counter, Dad prayed with me. I kissed him goodbye and headed to my gate. I found my seat, fastened the belt across my lap, and settled back for a quiet flight. But my flight was anything but quiet. I had so much to consider. One minute I imagined myself standing firm and resolute against Jim's charm, and the next I fantasized about running into his arms as we professed our undying love for one another and him telling me how much he loved Becky. *How wonderful that would be. But even if he made such a claim, can I believe he means it in his heart, or is he just trying to get me back?*

The wheels of the plane hit the tarmac with a thud, jolting me back to reality. I'd been totally lost in thought the entire way. I glanced toward the passenger seated beside me. "Wow! That was a rough landing. Must be a rookie pilot."

The man grinned and rolled his eyes.

Inside the terminal I gazed around, searching for the information screen. Spotting the bank of screens, I started toward it only to see an extremely tall man striding toward me, wearing a big smile and carrying a mountain of red roses. It was Steve. "Here." He thrust the flowers into my hands. "One dozen for each of the three months I've known you."

I was indignant. *Was there no getting away from this man? How did he know when I was flying and which plane I'd be on?* Dumping the flowers in the nearest trash can, I marched off toward the nearest restaurant to get a quick lunch before my next flight. My short legs were no match for his long strides. In no time he caught up with me.

"Oh, don't be mad at me," he pleaded. "I just wanted to make sure you were OK. And I just wanted to see you for a little while. I knew you had a two-hour layover." He cast me a sly little smile. "And I wouldn't want you to have to spend all that time by yourself."

Just inside the first restaurant I came to, I joined the line of customers waiting for a table. Stopping abruptly, I turned to face him. "Let me get this straight. Are you telling me that you flew all the way from Miami just to be here with me for my two-hour layover?"

"Yep, I sure did." He preened like a strutting peacock. "Better yet, you don't have to wait two hours. I can fly you to Dallas on my jet."

Now I was even more infuriated. The waitress led us to a table. He chose to sit across from me. After a quick glance at the menu we ordered our food, and the waitress left us alone.

I was so angry that I was in no mood for dinner conversation. Our food arrived, and we ate in silence. He was the first to speak.

"Don't you understand? I'm in love with you. I want to spend the rest of my life with you. I'm asking you to marry me!"

Enraged by his declaration of love, I was shaking. "Are you crazy? I don't love you. Why would you want to marry someone who doesn't even love you? I still love Jim."

"Oh, I can live with that. In time, you'll learn to love me. Besides, I can give you and Becky the kind of life that will make you happy. You'll never want for anything ever again." He reached across the table to capture my hands; I pulled away. "We will have such a wonderful life together, don't you see? I've never ever before met anyone like you!" He leaned back against the padded booth. "I'm telling you, it may not be today or tomorrow, or the next day or the next, but I am telling you that you will marry me sooner or later."

I leaped to my feet and pointed my finger in his face. "Steve, you cannot force me to marry you just because it's what you want. I'm telling you right now. I will never, never, never marry you! I don't love you, and I never will!" I gathered up my purse and my carry-on luggage and then pointed my finger in his face once more. "I'm not some alligator you can wrestle into submission. I want you out of my life! Leave me alone! Don't contact me ever again, not ever!"

I whirled about and stormed from the restaurant amid a sea of curious stares. He was right behind me, still pleading. I thought, *This man is crazy!*

"What part of No don't you understand?" As I neared my departure gate I was relieved to see passengers were already boarding the Dallas flight.

"One last time, Steve, leave me alone!" I whirled about and hurried into the jetway.

My hands were shaking as I read the seat numbers on each side of the plane's aisle.

As my gaze shifted from side to side on the plane, an attractive-looking man with silver hair caught my attention. He looked distinguished in his three-piece suit and had a briefcase resting on his lap. My heart skipped a beat, and the thought raced through my mind, *Hey, I'd like to sit next to a gentleman like him.* As it turned out, we were seated next to one another on opposite sides of the aisle. I smiled at him, wondering if he were a lawyer or a banker. *A professional, no doubt.*

He smiled back at me and returned to reading his *Wall Street Journal.* After fastening my seat belt, I glanced across the aisle once more. His nose was still stuck in the newspaper. I wondered, *Why am I so attracted to this man? How can I get his attention?*

I leaned across the aisle. "Sir? Excuse me, sir, but what did the captain say the temperature would be in Dallas today?" In all honesty, I had heard every word the captain said.

Glancing politely up from his newspaper he told me, "Seventy-two degrees."

I smiled to myself. *More like ninety-five and rising. . . . How can I keep him talking?* I sensed that he was only half listening to me and that he really wanted to return to the article he was reading. But I was determined.

"So, you're flying to Dallas?" I shot in a perky smile. *Duh! That was an intelligent conversation starter. Everyone on the plane is going to Dallas.*

"Uh, yes . . ." He smiled politely and went back to his paper.

"Me too. I'm flying down from my home in Michigan to take the Texas state boards for my RN degree. It's where I graduated from, and so it makes sense to . . ." I was babbling, and he was only half listening. But I kept going. "My five-year-old daughter, Becky, is staying with my folks until I return."

Suddenly he sat straight up and looked intently at me. "What was that you said?"

"You mean about my daughter Becky?"

He nodded. "Are you telling me that you have a daughter?"

I grinned with pleasure. "Yes, and she's absolutely adorable!"

"How old is she?"

"Almost five." I searched through my purse for my wallet. "Here! See!" I handed him a photo of Becky.

"That's not possible. You're not old enough to have a five-year-old. How old are you?"

"I'm twenty-five."

He vigorously shook his head in disbelief. "There's no way . . . I'm sorry, but I don't believe you." He eyed me critically. "Would you mind showing me your driver's license?"

I couldn't believe this man was carding me. I took my driver's license out of my wallet and handed it to him. Again he shook his head. "That's not possible. You don't look old enough to have a child. I apologize, but you are the youngest looking twenty-five-year-old I've ever seen. I thought you were sixteen. You look like a school girl."

In his defense, I had long straight hair that fell to my waist. I wore no makeup. And I was carrying a couple of my nursing books so that I could continue studying for my state boards while traveling.

We talked all the way to Dallas. I learned that his name was Tim Walsh and that he was single. He was the Central Region manager for a computer company and was based in Chicago. I was also beginning to get the feeling that our meeting on this flight was anything but chance. I'd changed my flight plans twice, and he'd changed his at least three times.

Since I'd never worked with a computer at the time, I was fascinated with everything he said. I loved to hear him talk. I was impressed with his intelligence. He seemed to know something about every subject I brought up. Whenever the flight attendant passed by, we dodged back and forth to maintain eye contact. A half-hour before the plane landed, I felt as though Tim was the answer to my prayer. *Is my attraction to this man a sign from God that I'm not supposed to meet Jim?* I wondered. Then the thought hit me, *I would like to marry a man like this.* That really surprised me because I thought I was still in love with Jim!

I do know that God leads in mysterious ways. It is very hard for me to explain why I had such a strong impression that Tim was the man for me. Perhaps it was because my family and I had prayed so earnestly that God should lead in this way. I only know that it was the strongest impression I've ever had. I know God doesn't work this way for everyone, and some could get confused because they are attracted by looks or position and get into a relationship without really getting to know the person's character. It is very important to get to know a person well—and to seek the Lord's will—before getting into a relationship.

Over the public address system, the flight attendant announced, "Please return your seats to an upright position and put your tray tables in place."

The wheels touched down on the runway.

Tim said suddenly, "If you aren't doing anything this evening, I would love to take you to dinner."

I couldn't believe my ears. "I'd love to."

Standing face to face in the aisle, he suggested that I choose the restaurant. I chose the one at the top of the Hyatt Regency Hotel. Tim said he'd pick me up at seven. He also asked for the phone number of where I'd be staying. I was not in the habit of giving out my phone number to strange men—especially after my experience with Steve. But somehow I felt completely safe with Tim. I quickly wrote down my friend Sherry's number on my ticket stub and handed it to him.

Sherry had been my roommate for a short while when we were both in nursing school. A dedicated Christian woman, she was a wonderful friend and had a soft heart. She had invited me to stay with her and her roommate for the night, and the next day we would drive to Austin together to take our nursing boards.

As my friend and confidant, Sherry knew all about my problem with Steve the stalker. She knew how relentless he was and how he'd had me followed. We'd even discussed what we would do if he followed us to Austin.

When Tim and I walked off the plane, I spotted Sherry and waved to her. "Come and meet my friend." I motioned for Tim to follow me. By the strange look on Sherry's face, I realized that she must think Tim was Steve because he had followed me off the plane. Being a little flustered

at the time and intent on figuring out how to let her know Tim wasn't
Steve, I blurted out an introduction. "Sherry, I'd like you to meet my
friend Steve." I then asked Sherry to give him directions to her apartment.

It never dawned on me that I had said Steve instead of Tim. And
Tim, not wanting to interrupt, just let it go. Sherry, thinking this was the
infamous Steve, purposely gave him the wrong directions to her place.
Tim and I said Goodbye.

Traveling with only a garment bag, he headed for the car rental of-
fices, and I headed for the luggage carousel to retrieve my suitcase. Ironi-
cally, it took Tim the same amount of time to secure his rental car as it
took me to find my suitcase. We passed each other as we drove out of the
airport. We waved and then turned in opposite directions.

"See that guy?" I took a deep breath and grinned. "That's the man I'm
going to marry!"

Sherry shot me a horrified look. "What? You're going to marry Steve?"

"No! I'm not talking about Steve. I'm talking about Tim."

Sherry, realizing her mistake, didn't have the heart to tell me that she
had given him the wrong directions. In a voice so quiet I had to ask her
to repeat herself, she muttered, "I don't think you're going to marry that
man."

I didn't know why Sherry was so doubtful. "Well, you never know
about these things," I said. "He just might be the one God has chosen for
me. Only time will tell. Hey, can you stop at the mall on the way? I want
to buy a new dress for my first date with my future husband," I teased.

I found the perfect dress, light blue, below the knee with a soft full-
ness in the skirt—not too fancy but not too casual. Perfect! When we
got back to Sherry's apartment I tried to call Jim but was unable to reach
him. I left a message saying I was very sorry but that I had second thoughts
about meeting with him. I told him that I loved him very much but I
didn't think it would be a good idea for us to see each other again. I
added that I wanted him to be happy and I hoped someday he would
find it in his heart to forgive me.

Somehow I knew I had made the right decision, and I was filled with
a sense of peace. I was just not strong enough to resist the man I had
loved so much.

Seven o'clock came and went. By seven-thirty I was getting nervous. Was Tim standing me up? To distract myself, I sat down at Sherry's piano and began to play. Happy or sad, I best express my emotions in my piano music.

It was almost eight o'clock when the phone rang. It was Tim. "Somehow I must have gotten your friend's directions wrong. I followed them to the apartment she gave, and two little old ladies answered and assured me that no Brenda Logan was there. Then I thought perhaps her apartment was in a matching building in the area. Another lady answered and assured me that no Brenda Logan was staying there."

"I'm so sorry."

"I thought I'd been had, that maybe you'd given me the wrong directions on purpose. But then I remembered that I had your phone number. I am so happy to hear your voice."

"I am so sorry for the confusion. Let me give you the correct directions to Sherry's apartment." A few minutes later I opened the door to a very relieved Tim.

The date, for me, could only be described as magical. The elegant circular restaurant had outside tables with a view of downtown Dallas. The floor turned while we ate, giving us a 360-degree view of the city. It was very romantic.

The waiter seated me and handed us menus. Tim's eyes sparkled with happiness. "Go ahead. Order whatever you like."

I ordered a salad and a baked potato.

"You need more than that. Order something else," he insisted.

"No, thank you. That's all I want." Being a vegetarian in the heart of cattle country didn't leave many choices on the menu, but I didn't care. Who could eat at a time like this?

Tim ordered a shrimp cocktail, a sirloin steak, a baked potato, and dessert. Since I hadn't ordered an appetizer, when his shrimp cocktail arrived he felt self-conscious eating it in front of me. He asked if I wanted some. When I declined, he insisted that I at least take a bite. I had never before tasted unclean meat. But rather than having to explain my reason for saying no and take a chance of getting into a biblical discussion on the topic, I took one shrimp—and swallowed it whole. A few days later, this act would come back to haunt me. But for the time being I had avoided what I thought might be an embarrassing situation for both of us.

We shared a good laugh over the mix-up in Sherry's directions. That's when Tim told me that he'd cancelled a dinner invitation at his boss's house that evening. "I told him I'd met a beautiful girl on the plane and could he get me out of dinner. John just looked at me in disbelief. 'Donna is going to kill me,' he said. 'She's worked all day on the menu. You're going to owe me big time for this one.'"

We sat side by side and laughed together as if we'd known each other for years. I hung on to his every word. He told me about his work projects. We talked about world events, history, politics, and just about everything but religion. I couldn't believe how much this man knew. I was impressed with his kind and gentle manner, and I liked the way he seemed genuinely interested in what I had to say. I was having such a good time I didn't want the evening to end.

Later that night while I was getting ready for bed, I thought back over the past three months and all I had been through—the breakup with Jim and the stalking with Steve. It had left my heart and nerves raw.

My mind still struggled with my decision concerning Jim. I longed to tell him it was all a misunderstanding and that it would somehow work out for us. But I knew that wasn't true.

Yet now, strangely, I felt a sense of contentment, something I hadn't felt in months. It was as if God had brought Tim into my life to say, "Brenda, trust Me and I will give you the desire of your heart." New hope welled up within me.

Looking back almost thirty years now, I have only one regret. When Jim first mentioned he didn't want to be called Daddy, I wish I had asked him why. I wish we had discussed his feelings about Becky so that I would have understood better his lack of bonding with her. I was just too afraid he would say almost anything to get me to marry him. I was afraid he would talk me out of what I knew in my heart was the right thing to do.

Maybe trust was the major issue. I knew I didn't trust myself—I loved Jim too much. And after my experiences with Dave and then Steve, I had a hard time trusting men at all. The easiest thing to do was to withdraw, to refuse Jim's phone calls and refuse to meet with him in Dallas.

However, as my trust in God has increased over the years, I have learned that God can give me the strength I need in order to stand up for what I believe. I no longer have to be afraid to say what's on my heart; I no longer have to do things that compromise my standards—like eating shrimp! I no longer have to be dishonest in my relationships. I can share my true feelings.

I now know that if God didn't want me to marry Jim, He could have made it clear to both of us if we had just talked things through. Withholding information almost always hurts someone, even if it's done with the best intentions!

And what did I learn from my encounters with Steve? I was very fortunate that Steve only stalked me. He could have been a dangerous criminal! I should never have shared my deep emotional feelings with a stranger. This obviously made Steve feel connected with me, even though I had no feelings for him. I know now that when a man meets a woman's emotional needs, he often expects a sexual payoff!

I also learned that it's not a good idea to accept gifts, especially expensive ones. It can be a man's way of "buying" a woman. Steve probably thought that I owed him something since he went out of his way to purchase first-class tickets, roses, and the stereo—and with persistence he thought he was going to get it. He probably hoped that I would begin to feel obligated to him and give in. I'm just glad he didn't take what he wanted by force. God was so good to protect me!

Finding the Love of My Life

It's not easy to sit back and wait on the Lord. And you're probably thinking at this point that I wasn't exactly sitting back and waiting when I spotted a distinguished looking man on the plane and started up a conversation with him. All I know is that in God's own time, if we trust, He will give us the desires of our heart. He knows far better than we do what it is that will bring to us the abundant life that He died to give us.

And so I held on to Psalm 37:3–5:

Trust in the LORD, and do good. . . .
Delight yourself also in the LORD,
And He shall give you the desires of your heart.

Commit your way to the LORD,
Trust also in Him,
And He shall bring it to pass (NKJV).

Read on as I share how God brought me the desire of my heart.

CHAPTER II

Beginning Again

Tim returned to Chicago the next day but called me on the phone. In fact he called every night while I was in Dallas. We talked for hours about everything, including religion. After a long day of taking exams, I couldn't wait for his call. During one of our late-night talks, we broached the Bible subject of eating unclean meats. His response was adamant. "I don't believe it. I've never heard of any such law."

"Do you have a Bible close by?"

"Yes."

"Go get it." While I waited for him to return to the phone I prayed for wisdom.

"OK, I have the Bible."

"Turn to the book of Leviticus." I directed him to chapter 11. He read the words aloud. I could hear the stunned surprise in his voice.

"I have never read that before. Hey! In the restaurant I coaxed you to try a bite of my shrimp."

"Yes . . ."

"Why did you do it if you knew it was wrong?"

Wow! Talk about hitting it head-on. I attempted to explain. "I didn't want to embarrass you with a discussion of unclean meat when you had just ordered the shrimp cocktail. I felt terrible after I ate it. I couldn't even bring myself to chew it, so I swallowed it whole. My conscience bothered me for some time after that. And now I'm embarrassed that I didn't stand up for what I knew was right." *When will I learn to trust God and not try to do things my way?*

"Whoa!" He fell silent for a moment. "Brenda, I will never ever again force you to do anything you don't want to do. I promise. And if eating unclean meat is wrong, I'll never touch the stuff again."

We had spent so much time talking on the phone that we had grown close in a short amount of time. Somehow, I just felt in my heart that I would marry this man. I didn't know how God was going to work out our differences in religious beliefs, but Tim was so open to Bible truth, such as the unclean meat issue, that I wasn't really worried. Instead, I kept this concern before the Lord, trusting that He would work it out in His own time.

One night when our conversation moved from various topics to more romantic territory, Tim commented, "I really miss you. Sure wish you could come home sooner than two weeks." The yearning I heard in his voice, I too felt.

I paused for a moment. I was almost finished taking my boards. I had planned to visit with friends for a week before returning home, but it would be nice to be with Becky again. And I did miss Tim—almost as much as he vowed he missed me. Also I had promised my father that I would never again marry a man of whom he didn't approve. If Tim was the man I was to marry, perhaps having my father meet Tim as soon as possible would be a good idea. In fact, with things moving as fast as they were between us, the sooner the better.

"All right—if you'll agree to meet my family when I get there."

"Consider it done!"

I scheduled my flight immediately following my last exam. As I dis-embarked from my plane in Chicago, butterflies flitted wildly in my stomach. Tim met me at the gate with a huge smile on his face and a bouquet of flowers in his hand. One look at his rapturous smile and I had no doubt but that I was falling in love with this man and he with me.

That evening we had dinner with Tim's best friend, Frank, and his wife, Doris. While I was nervous to meet them, they welcomed me gra-ciously. Later I learned that when I left the table for the ladies' room Frank told Tim, "You'd better hang on to this one."

As Tim and I drove through Hinsdale, we stopped at the house of my friends, Jim and Terrilee Jenks. We had sung together in a singing group called The Way while I attended Southern Missionary College, and I had been a bridesmaid at their wedding. Jim was an obstetrician and Terrilee a nurse. I was eager to see what they thought of Tim. At one point Terrilee took me into the kitchen. "Brenda, you are perfect for each other. He obviously adores you! You really have a winner this time." I couldn't have been happier. But the important opinions were yet to come, that of my daughter and my parents.

It was during our drive to my folks' place in Alma, Michigan, that our relationship met its first major hurdle.

"By the way, what does your father do?"

"He's a preacher."

He glanced over at me. "I'm sorry. I couldn't hear you. What did you say he does?"

I repeated myself, a little louder this time.

Tim broke into laughter. "OK, now what does he really do?"

I frowned and cast him a serious look. "He really is a preacher."

Tim blinked and stared at the road ahead. "You're serious, huh?"

I nodded.

"What denomination?"

I answered without hesitation. "Seventh-day Adventist."

Suddenly he slammed on the brakes and pulled off to the side of the road. He turned toward me, his face solemn. "I once knew some Seventh-day Adventists. They were very strict. They didn't drink or smoke or dance, or, basically, do anything fun!" He looked me straight in the eyes. "This is not going to work!"

"Oh, Tim, my parents are wonderful people. And I can assure you, Daddy will not try to shove religion down your throat. Actually my father is a very funny guy. Everyone loves him. I know you'll like him too." While I thought I'd partly convinced him, I knew he was still far from being won over. Later I learned that at that moment, in Tim's mind, our relationship was over. All I can say is, God must have known what Tim needed and inspired my folks to love and accept him just the way he was, and let God work out the rest!

At my folks' place, things couldn't have gone better. Mom and Dad welcomed Tim warmly into their home, and Becky was very excited to meet him. The minute he sat down, she climbed up into his lap and gave him a big hug. The remark that followed left all of us speech-

Brenda and Tim during his first visit to her parents' home.

less.

"Oh, Daddy," Becky innocently said, "you're here!"

"Let me get everyone something to drink," Mom said, trying to change the subject.

The most shocked person of all was Tim, but he didn't correct Becky. From then on she only called him Daddy. Tim stayed with us for the weekend, and everyone loved him.

Unbelievable! My father had never liked one boyfriend I brought home—ever! *Now if only Tim would give his heart to Jesus, everything would be perfect!* "Lord," I prayed, "if You have chosen Tim to be my husband, please let Your Holy Spirit work on his heart."

After all the excitement over meeting Tim had died down, Mom waved a copy of the *Detroit News* in my face. "Look what came in the mail while you were gone!" she said. She had a big smile on her face as she handed me the newspaper. It was dated February 11, 1979. Tim looked over my shoulder as I read a letter on the editorial page called "Contact 10."

A snowmobile accident near Houghton Lake tore open my upper lip quite badly, and my friends rushed me to the Mercy Hospital emergency room in Grayling, Michigan. The injury was severe enough that a specialist was required, so Mercy Hospital rendered first aid and sent me immediately down to Beaumont Hospital for treatment by a plastic surgeon. I'm doing quite well, thank you, but I can't forget the first person I met at Mercy Hospital, a nurse whose attitude and bedside manner were, I feel, exemplary. Even as a surgeon at Belmont was operating, I couldn't stop thinking about the pretty little blue-eyed Florence Nightingale, but I don't know her name, and I doubt the hospital would release it—so I could send flowers and a card. My only clue is that she signed my release form with the initials "B. L."

Signed, B. S. Warren

The *Detroit News* replied:

Everyone we talked to at Mercy immediately knew B. L.'s identity, but you're right, it's against hospital policy to release her full name. Your favorite nurse, we learned, hails from Dallas and is on a temporary leave of absence, but she'll return in a couple of weeks. Mercy's spokesman told us it's also against official policy for any of the hospital personnel to accept gratuities of any kind.

That being said, another authority suggested that in a couple of weeks, a card might be sent along with a box of candy. The card will be placed in the emergency room bulletin board for all to share and, he said, "Everyone will get a pat on the back" when the candy is opened. He suggested that you simply address the package to Ms. B. L., R.N. Emergency Room, Mercy Hospital, 1100 Michigan, Grayling, MI 49738.

Don't forget to include your name and address and perhaps, just perhaps, you'll get a signed thank you with her full name. We also suspect that a single yellow rose for this lovely Texas lady would not be deemed a horrifying breach of policy.

After reading the article, my parents, as well as Tim, were interested in hearing the story behind the article. I explained, "Just before I left for Texas, this patient injured in a snowmobile accident came into the ER. His upper lip had been torn up, and he was bleeding badly. Frightened and not able to talk because of his injuries, I stayed with him and held pressure on his wounds to control the bleeding, while the medical staff made arrangements to transport him to a specialist near Detroit.

"He seemed so distraught that I asked him if he would like for me to pray with him. He nodded. I prayed that the Lord would be his Great Physician, that God would take away his fear and give him peace. I also prayed that he would give his heart to the Lord, to make that decision right there as no one can guarantee tomorrow.

"When I opened my eyes, tears were running down his face. I held his hand, and he squeezed it. I gave him another shot for the pain and continued to talk with him. Slowly his facial muscles relaxed as his fear and pain subsided. When the ambulance arrived that would take him to Detroit, I walked alongside the stretcher, escorting him to the waiting vehicle. Just before they lifted him into the ambulance, he stretched out his hand. I took it in mine. Tears welled up in his eyes. He squeezed my hand and then he was taken away, and I returned to the ER."

The next week a delivery of flowers came to the ER, not a single yellow rose but two dozen of the most beautiful yellow roses I'd ever seen. With it came a five-pound box of Godiva chocolates, and a note with the man's name and phone number. I called and thanked him for the flowers and the candy. My patient turned out to be a wealthy man. He owned a huge carpet company in Detroit. He told me that if I ever needed anything—ever—all I had to do was call.

"I'm sure glad I met you before he did," Tim teased after the roses and candy arrived.

During the weeks that followed, Tim and I couldn't see enough of one another. Not a day went by that we didn't talk on the phone at least once, and often two or three times. While at work he'd call for just a few minutes to tell me he was thinking of me. In the evening we'd talk for hours. He would tell me about different businesses with which he had to deal, and I would tell him about my patients. Every weekend he'd either drive or fly up from Chicago to see me.

Becky was just as excited as I was to see her "Daddy." Often when Tim arrived for the weekend she'd run into his arms faster than I could. Then she would insist he come see her Barbie dolls or play horsy with her. I could see a bond developing between them almost overnight. Whether we went for a walk in the woods, a trip to the store, or a dinner date, wherever we went, Becky went too.

At this time I was still living with my sister Linda at Camp Au Sable in Michigan. Though our one-room attic apartment was incredibly small, it holds some of my fondest memories. I had made a toy area for Becky's things, complete with a toy stove and refrigerator made out of cardboard boxes. She would "cook" in her little kitchen while I cooked in mine. I divided the room with larger pieces of furniture for privacy. While Becky and I didn't have a bed, we slept together on a mattress on the floor.

A few weeks after we met Tim, Becky and I spent the weekend at my parents' home. I was in the kitchen helping Mom with the dishes while Tim and Dad talked in the parlor. I glanced in and then turned to my mother. "They seem to really like each other. I am so glad. Tim told me that he really likes you both."

"That's good. We'd better hurry if we want to go over to the Alma church to practice for tomorrow." Mom seemed to be trying to give them some privacy.

Mom and I were singing special music for church, and I was to play the organ for the services. While we were practicing, Dad and Tim continued their conversation. I was dying of curiosity but sensed I should wait for one of them to volunteer information concerning what they were talking about. But neither one said a word. Several months passed before I found out how important their conversations really were.

CHAPTER 12

Midwinter Romance

I eyed my straight brown hair critically. The weight of the waist-length hair ruined my determined attempts at producing curls. I gave the sides of my hair an extra pouf and one more spritz of hair spray. Turning first one way and then the other in front of the full-length mirror, I examined every inch of my new blue-and-white flowered dress from the neckline to the hem. I loved the way my heels coordinated with the dress. Everything had to be perfect!

I glanced out the window at the sunlight sparkling on the lake. I loved the way the sunlight wafted through the limbs of the tall evergreens. What a lovely beginning for a magical weekend together! My heart skipped a beat as I glanced at my watch. It was time for me to leave to pick up Tim at the airport in Traverse City, an hour away. I'd been anticipating his visit all week long. Even though I would have to work my shifts at the hospital while he was there, I knew our time together would be special.

It had been three months since Tim and I met on that memorable flight to Dallas. The previous weekend he'd told me he loved me. I knew "I love you" wasn't something he said lightly.

It was time to go meet him, and in my haste to see him again, I didn't think to grab a coat or scarf when I left the house, nor did I think to turn off the house lights. Halfway to the airport, the first tiny snowflake splattered against my windshield.

"Oh, great! Just what I need! A snowstorm! I hope his plane isn't late." I said a quick prayer asking God to let him land safely. By the time I reached the airport the tiny snow flurries had escalated into heavy, wet snow with a driving wind.

Coatless, I hopped out of the car, ran inside the terminal, and checked the list of arrivals, only to discover that Tim's plane would indeed be late. And I was early. I wandered into the waiting area and planted myself in view of the gate where his plane was scheduled to land.

By now the snow was falling hard and fast, swirling about the runways beyond the bank of windows. Would Tim's plane be able to land? I didn't want to consider the possibility that he might not arrive. I'd planned our every moment together. I sensed he might even ask me to marry him after last week's declaration of love. Everything had to be perfect!

When the voice of the female ticket agent came over the loudspeaker, I held my breath. "Flight number 174 from Detroit has landed and is approaching Gate 7." I broke into a smile, gave a little cheer, and jumped to my feet. As I watched the passengers exit the jetway, I nervously smoothed out my skirt. Finally Tim appeared and waved to me. My smile widened as I sprang into his arms. He gave me a huge hug and then told me all about the rough ride he'd had.

"It was the first time since I've been flying that I really questioned whether or not I'd safely make it!"

I hugged him tighter. He then eyed my dress and shoes.

"Where's your coat? It's a blizzard out there."

"I know, but when I left the house the air was warm and the sun was shining. In fact, it was so warm out, it never occurred to me to bring a coat! After all, we are only an hour from the airport!" *Who could have predicted such a freak snowstorm? I wish I had watched the weather report.*

I snuggled up beside him as we walked toward the luggage carousel. By the time he retrieved his bags and we headed outside, the snow was falling so heavily that we could barely make out the cars in the parking area.

"I can't believe you forgot to wear your coat." He eyed my shoes and shook his head. "How are you going to run through the snow in those high heels? You'll kill yourself!" His gentle scolding made me feel even more protected. I couldn't believe how fast the storm had swept into the area.

As Tim drove the hour-long ride to Grayling, the visibility was so poor that we couldn't make out the lines in the middle of the road. Night fell. Ice kept jamming the windshield wipers. I asked Tim if he minded if I prayed. I felt we were in danger and needed God's protection. From time to time I had to stick my head out the window so that I could tell Tim where the edge of the road was. At the entrance to Camp Au Sable, we slid to a stop. The accumulation of snow was so deep the car would go no farther.

With Jim and Linda's house at least a mile from the entrance, there wasn't much we could do but walk. We left the suitcases in the car, locked it up, and started off in the direction of their house. Tim tried to give me his jacket; but I insisted he wear it. Locking his arm about me, he tried to protect me from the cold. Between the falling snow and the darkness of night I couldn't tell if we were on the road or wandering off in some field or wetland. It seemed as though we'd walked forever.

"Tim, I can't go on. My side hurts terribly; I can barely walk." I doubled over and pressed my clenched fist into my hurting side.

"Brenda, you have to go on. We can't stay here. We'll freeze to death!"

Gasping through the pain, I shook my head. The tears were freezing on my cheeks. "You go on; I'll catch up with you later."

"Don't be silly. I'm not leaving you out here alone."

By now, ten inches of heavy, wet snow covered the ground. My feet were so numb I could no longer feel them.

"I can't go on! I know I can't!" I was in the middle of urging him to leave me behind once again, when he spotted a light from a window up ahead. "Look! It can't be far, honey. You can make it!"

No beam of light had ever seemed as warm or inviting as the light shining from the tiny window in my upstairs loft. He scooped me close to his side and propelled me through the last few yards of snow to Jim and Linda's house. By God's grace we'd made it home safely.

Once inside, we knelt to pray and thank God for His traveling mercy. Then Tim ran cold water into the tub and insisted I put my feet in the water. Even the cold water felt warm. If we had been out in the cold snow much longer, I would have had frostbite. Slowly and patiently he added more warmth to the water until I could feel life in my toes once again.

The next morning I arose early to bake fresh bread in my sister's kitchen. Outside the kitchen window was a sparkling winter wonderland, like a card from Currier & Ives. Snow clung to every tree limb and branch. White blanketed every building. I stepped outside for a better look and inhaled the magic of the freshly fallen snow.

Returning to the kitchen, I turned on the radio to a local news station and learned that almost fifty cars had been stranded along the same road we'd been on. The hospital called, informing me that my shift had been cancelled. Another nurse would cover for me. This left the entire day for Tim and me to enjoy together. I fixed dinner ahead of time so that I would only need to warm it up. I hummed my favorite summer-camp chorus as I rolled out the dough for Tim's favorite dessert—cherry pie.

"Isn't it beautiful?" Tim came into the kitchen and slipped his arms about my waist. "Let's take a walk."

"Wearing the proper coats and boots, right?" I looked up at him and grinned.

He planted a kiss on the tip of my nose. "Absolutely."

I patted his cheek. "I'll put on my coat and boots while the pie finishes baking."

Minutes later, with the cherry pie cooling on the pie rack, we strolled arm in arm through the magical winter paradise. It was cold, but not the biting cold of the previous night, and we walked and talked about God's care on the drive home from the airport. I could see that Tim was yearning for a closer walk with God. As a child he had attended church only a couple of times. Tim's parents were not regular members of any church, and although he had been introduced to various religions while in the navy, he had never given his heart to Jesus. Before we met, he spent quite a bit of time studying the Bible. His life was empty, and he was searching for something better—he just didn't know what. He loved what he saw in our family. He told me that our family was special and he knew it was because of God.

At the Cedar Lodge, we stepped inside to get warm and found a cozy fire going in the fireplace. Tim smiled at my look of surprise. *So that's where he's been while I was baking the bread,* I thought. *No wonder he's been acting a little nervous this morning.* After shedding my coat I gravitated toward the piano. I sat down and played a few of my favorite songs while Tim made himself comfortable on a nearby sofa. I continued singing as he got up from the sofa, walked to the big picture window and, for some time, stared out at the snow. Suddenly I knew; he was going to ask me to marry him. I walked up behind him and slipped my arms around him. He turned to face me.

Brenda and Tim in the Cedar Lodge, newly engaged.

"Brenda, there's something I want to ask you." He looked serious; his voice cracked. He cleared his throat.

"Honey, just tell me what it is."

"Brenda, I have fallen in love with you, and I can't imagine my life without you. I'm asking you to marry me and be my wife. I want to adopt Becky as my daughter. I want us to be a family!"

Before he could get out the rest of his rehearsed speech I threw my arms around his neck. "Yes! Yes, I'll marry you!"

It had taken him three months to say that he loved me and now only a week later he was asking me to be his wife. I was ecstatic! I needed no time to think about it. I had known in my heart for some time now that Tim was the man I had been praying for.

Arm in arm we walked back to Linda's house, bonded in a way we'd never before experienced. Four words, "Will you marry me?" changed everything. I couldn't wait to get back to the house and call my family. I called Becky first.

"Honey, Daddy and I are getting married."

"Really?" Her excitement erupted through the telephone wires. She spoke with Tim and then came back on the line to speak with me. "Mommy, can I wear a wedding dress?"

I hadn't thought as far ahead as to the kind of wedding we'd have. "Sure, honey, sure."

Next I called my parents. How different this call was from the call I made for my first marriage. My folks were thrilled. I knew they liked Tim, but I was a little surprised that they were so supportive of our marriage. After all, he was not a Seventh-day Adventist. In my mind, I just knew he would be—and that was enough for me. I felt that God had brought us together and God would take care of the rest!

I realize now that I probably should have waited to make wedding plans until after I had assurance that God was working a miracle in Tim's heart. But at the time, I was learning step by step to depend on God. I was taking baby steps in my new relationship with Christ. I was trying not to run ahead of the Lord, but it was difficult! I felt in my heart I was making the right decision, and my folks approved. That was enough for me!

Mom and Dad had grown to love and respect Tim. Better yet, they knew he loved Becky *and* me and that he would be a good husband and father. After hanging up from the last of my calls to my brothers and sisters, I prepared dinner while Tim started a fire in the fireplace. We sat cross-legged on the floor in front of the fireplace to eat our dinner and enjoy the cozy atmosphere.

When we finished dinner we gathered the dinnerware and placed it in the sink to be washed. "I have something to show you," I said mysteriously.

"What is it?" His eyes twinkled with happiness.

"Wait right here!" I dashed up the stairs to my tiny apartment and returned minutes later with my hand behind my back.

His eyes narrowed; he pursed his lips. "What do you have there?"

I opened my hand slowly, revealing a gold name pin. He took it from me and read the inscription, "Mrs. Brenda Walsh, R.N." A smile spread across his face. "How long have you had this?"

I felt a little sheepish. "I ordered it from an ad in one of my nursing magazines. It arrived three weeks ago, nine weeks after I'd placed the order."

Tim threw back his head and laughed, and then drew me into his arms. "I didn't have a chance, did I?"

I shook my head.

Giving me another bear hug he exclaimed, "You are adorable—downright adorable! And I love you!"

We stayed up late that night watching the moon come up over the snow-covered lake and shimmering on the branches of the trees. We talked about our future life together and about how important it was to make God first in our lives. I shared with him my dream of having a Christian husband that would be a spiritual leader in our home. I told him how I always felt sorry for the women in our church who sat alone with their children because their husbands didn't believe in God. He assured me that we would have a Christian home and that he wanted to be a good father to Becky and that he had every intention of being right there next to me on the pew each Sabbath. I was amazed at his knowledge and acceptance of so many of the Seventh-day Adventist beliefs. He hadn't eaten unclean meat since our first date! He had no trouble accepting the seventh day as Sabbath or any of the other doctrines that I had talked with him about. I had no doubt in my mind that he would become a Seventh-day Adventist. I tried hard to be patient and not try and do the work of the Holy Spirit!

"I would really like to have a church wedding. Last time I really didn't care, but this time it means so much to me. I would love to have Becky be my flower girl." I took a deep breath, allowing the memories of childhood to resurrect within my imagination. "I want bridesmaids, flowers—the works!"

"You plan whatever wedding you want. It's fine with me." He kissed my forehead. "Honey, I promise to spend the rest of my life making you happy. I love you with all my heart!"

I snuggled down in the crook of his arm.

"My life was so empty before I met you. I am the luckiest man in the world!"

We set our wedding date six months from the time we met. Mom patiently took me all over Michigan to find the perfect wedding dress. We found one in Saginaw, Michigan. The minute I tried it on and stepped in front of the mirror, I knew it was the one for me. Ivory satin and lace with long sleeves and a long train—I felt like a princess. It took my breath away.

"I don't want to take it off," I said to my mother. I felt like a first-time bride.

My mom's eyes twinkled with tears. "Then it's the right one!"

I asked my aunt Myrtle, a professional cake decorator, to make our cake. Since high school I'd imagined that my favorite aunt would make my cake. While many of the wedding details had changed in my mind since high school days, the cake had not.

As we worked through plans for the wedding, reception, bridesmaid dresses, gown fittings, flowers, and addressing and mailing invitations, the next few months flew by. Two weeks before the wedding, Tim, Becky, and I spent the weekend with Mom and Dad. Mom and I had just finished washing and putting away the Friday-night dinner dishes. Mom went to her room to work on her Sabbath School program for the next day, and Dad was in his office working on his sermon. Tim had just finished reading a story to Becky and had tucked her into bed.

I kissed Becky good night, turned off the overhead light, and then walked into the parlor and joined Tim on the sofa. He slipped his arm around my shoulders. He seemed agitated about something. Before I could ask him what was wrong, he said, "Honey, I have something I need to tell you."

I panicked at the tone of his voice. What was wrong? Was he calling off the wedding two weeks ahead? The invitations are mailed. What would I do? I could see he was struggling to tell me something, but what?

"Tim, what is it? Please, whatever it is, you need to come right out and tell me."

"Brenda, I've decided that tomorrow I want to be baptized."

Now my head was spinning. I went from instant relief to elation. It was wonderful that he wanted to be baptized, and yet I felt he hadn't a clue what that decision entailed. But I threw my arms around him and gave him an excited hug.

He laughed. "I have never been so thoroughly hugged before I met you. You are the hugging-est family I've ever met. And I like it."

"Honey, I think it's wonderful that you want to be baptized tomorrow, but it doesn't quite work that way." Determined to explain just how baptism works, I gently patted his chest. "You don't just decide one day to be baptized and then be baptized the next day. You will need to study Seventh-day Adventism to be certain you understand . . ."

"Honey, you don't understand . . ."

"No, you don't understand, you have to . . ."

Gently he put his hand over my mouth. "Honey, please listen to me. I've been studying with your father for the past three months."

My mouth dropped open in surprise. "I didn't know. You never said . . ."

"I didn't say anything because I didn't want you to get your hopes up that I would join your church. I only asked your father for studies because if you were going to become my wife, I wanted to know what you believed. I didn't think for a moment that I would actually want to join your church."

I stared at him, speechless.

"But your dad introduced me to Jesus." Tim's eyes watered; his voice broke. "He took me to Calvary, and when I really understood what Jesus did for me, well . . ." He swallowed hard. "I've given my life to Jesus. I want to spend the rest of my life doing what Jesus wants me to do. I want us to have a truly Christian home. I want to be a Christian father to Becky and a Christian husband to you. I've asked for baptism, and your father is going to baptize me tomorrow."

I fell into his arms—sobbing tears, not of sadness but of joy. God had answered my prayer—again. He heard my cry, healed my heart, and blessed me more abundantly than I could have ever asked or imagined. With tears streaming down both of our faces we prayed together. We rededicated our lives to Him. We asked God to be the Head of our home and to lead in our lives.

Tim told me more about the Friday night a few weeks after we met when Mom and I had gone over to the church to practice for the Sabbath services. "While you were rehearsing, your dad and I were talking. I told your father that I wanted to 'come clean.' I told him I was very interested in his daughter and that if anything I told him he couldn't live with, I wanted to know right away and I'd back away from the relationship."

"Your dad was so patient with me. I told him everything bad I'd ever done. When I finished, your father told me how he'd been in the army

Tim, Brenda, and Pastor Micheff on the day of Tim's baptism.

and would drink and get into terrible fights before he knew Christ. And then he said, 'You know, Tim, God can forgive all that. It's going forward every day from here on out that matters. You just need to ask God to forgive you and He will.' That really touched my heart."

The next day I choked up as I watched my father lead my husband-to-be into the baptismal tank. Even Dad choked up so that he could hardly speak. As my father lowered Tim into the water I recalled our first meeting and then our first trip to my folks' home when Tim asked what my father did for a living and then determined in his mind that our relationship would go no further. But God had other plans.

CHAPTER 13

We Are a Family

Tim's strong baritone voice filled the packed church as he recited the vows he'd written to me. "At this moment here on earth, in heaven and forever, standing here before God, Jesus, our loved ones, and all my fellow men, I, Tim Walsh, take you, Brenda, as my wife, and Becky as my daughter."

My eyes welled up with tears at the mention of my daughter. Somehow I managed to swallow the sob rising to my throat. The day was beautiful, absolutely perfect. Our only moment of panic came when my academy roommate, Jan Nourollahi, called to say her flight was cancelled, leaving her stuck in Georgia. Fortunately Sharon, Tim's secretary, was about the same size and was willing to stand in for Jan as one of the five bridesmaids. I missed having my sister Cinda at the wedding, but she couldn't afford the airfare from California, where she was living at the time.

Out of the corner of my eye I could see my sister Linda, the matron of honor, standing beside Becky, the flower girl. My daughter had looked so adorable walking beside her cousin Jimmy, dropping petals as she walked. I could feel their happiness for me and for Tim.

Tim continued with his vows. "I will love you forever, always expressing to you the excitement, joy, and happiness that I feel from the love in my heart that God has given me to express. With the help of God I will forever provide you with all the necessities of this world, protecting us from harm, and sickness, caring for you in times of need, and forever to be with you in all things."

As I held his hands and stood face to face with him, I could feel him tremble with emotion as he spoke. I longed to wipe away the bead of sweat on his brow but feared I would distract him from his task. "I will bring love, happiness, joy, and excitement to our home and to all things that we do together. I will share with you my concerns so that with the help of God we can always do the right thing to do His will. With all the love in my heart I promise these things to you."

When Tim finished reciting his vows, he smiled at me through a wash of tears.

It was my turn. To be safe, I'd written my vows on the back of my favorite photograph of Tim. Dad had it in the cover of his Bible so he could prompt me if I became too nervous to remember what I'd written. Just knowing it was there, should I need it, gave me confidence. The only nerves I felt were from the excitement of the moment. I had no reservations and no second thoughts.

Front row, seated on floor, Rita Showers, Gail Micheff, Sharon Smith
Second row, kneeling, Frank Mako, flower girl Becky Walsh, Bible boy Jimmy Johnson, Al Pillarelli
Back row: Jim Johnson, Linda Johnson, Brenda Walsh, Tim Walsh, Sherry Stephenson,
John Mitchell, Jim Micheff, Jr.

"I, Brenda, take you, Tim, to be my husband, loving you now and forever. I will love you when we are together and when we are apart. I will respect you, trust and care for you through the best and worst of what is to come.

"I will honor your goals and dreams and help you fulfill them. I promise to be faithful to you, sharing my thoughts and experiences, always being open and honest. I pledge to you the rest of my life as your wife, your lover, and your friend. I say these things believing that God is in the midst of it all."

Turning toward my father, we knelt to pray. Tim squeezed my hand tight and began to pray. "Dear heavenly Father, thank You for bringing Brenda and Becky into my life. Since we met, You have blessed us with so much, most of all, love for You and each other. I ask that You will continue to bless us and our family, for us to know Your will so that we may serve You as You wish. I ask that You bless these vows that I have expressed today to give me the wisdom and strength to fulfill them to the fullest as You would expect. In the name of Jesus Christ, amen."

Dad's hands covered both of ours. "Dear heavenly Father," I prayed, "how can I thank You for bringing Tim into my life?" The tears that I had successfully contained now spilled out from me. My voice choked; I couldn't continue. Without missing a beat, my father picked up the prayer as if it had been planned, asking God for a special blessing on our lives, for God to stay close to us, and that we would always make Him first in our home.

My father pronounced us husband and wife, and Tim and I shared a sweet, tender kiss.

Dad placed his hand on Tim's shoulder and gave me a wide grin. He then looked out over the audience. "I now have the pleasure of introducing to you, Mr. and Mrs. Tim Walsh." I am sure there wasn't a dry eye in the audience. Family and friends knew I'd been a single mom. Everyone had heard the story of how Tim and I had met. And they were touched by the love Tim had not only for me but for Becky as well. The organist played the first triumphant chord of the recessional and, hand in hand, we fairly ran down the aisle of the church, eager to begin our new life together.

Aunt Myrtle's cake was the centerpiece of our simple reception. Pink and white roses matching my bouquet topped the four-tiered cake. A bevy of bridesmaids in sky blue chiffon dresses with a faint floral print satin underneath swirled around to congratulate us. Each had carried a single pink rose to complement my bouquet of pink and white roses.

Becky loved helping us open presents. Several times she came over to Tim and gave him a hug. "I love you so much, Daddy!" This brought tears to Tim's eyes and mine. For years after, Becky would show people our wedding album and say, "This is the day that we married Daddy."

The wedding of Tim and Brenda, with the cake made by Aunt Myrtle.

A silver stretch limousine carried Tim and me to the airport, where we boarded a plane for Carmel-by-the-Sea, California, for our week-long honeymoon, where we enjoyed strolling along the beach, shopping in the quaint shops, and dining in romantic restaurants.

While we were gone, Becky stayed with my sister Linda. Though we could have honeymooned longer, I hated being away from Becky for more than a week. On the first day of our honeymoon, Tim suggested we call Becky. "I want to be sure she's not missing us too much," he said.

After I spoke with Becky, my sister came on the line. "This morning Becky said she wanted to help me fix dinner. When I was ready to begin, Becky was down at the docks with Jim, so I called Becky's name over the loud speaker. 'Will Rebecca Lynn Logan please report to the kitchen right away?'

"A few minutes later Becky stomped into the kitchen and blurted out, 'Auntie, I am not Rebecca Lynn Logan. I just got married. My name is Rebecca Lynn Walsh. Don't ever call me that again!'"

After our honeymoon we drove to Michigan to pick up Becky. It was time to begin our lives together as a family. As we rode along the interstate, I studied Tim's profile in wonder. I couldn't believe it. He hadn't raised his hand to strike me, not even once. I really had married a prince!

Early in our courtship I'd told Tim that I probably could never have children. Soon after Becky was born I'd been diagnosed with cervical cancer and had received radiation therapy but had refused a hysterectomy. The doctors had done their best to talk me into it. "The radiation alone will make you sterile. Instead of worrying about having more children, you should be concerned with saving your life."

At the time I thought that as I was a single mother and still young, I couldn't possibly give up any hope of having a baby with my future husband, whoever he might be. After much prayer I chose not to have the surgery. When I told Tim about my condition, he couldn't have been sweeter.

"Well, before I met Becky, I thought I'd never really enjoy being a father. And now, she's really all I need to fulfill my life as a father." I loved him very much for that.

We'd been married only a few months when I noticed that my stomach seemed bigger. Immediately I thought, *The cancer's back.* I ran my hand across my abdomen and felt a rather large lump. Terrified, I recalled the doctor's words:

"If the cancer returns, you will probably have less than six months to live."

It couldn't have come at a worse time. Tim had been promoted as the western regional manager for educational services for Digital Equipment Corporation. We were planning to move to San Jose, California.

That night I lay awake beside Tim long after he'd fallen asleep, and I cried out to God. "Lord, You have given me a wonderful husband and a wonderful father for Becky. Please don't let me die now. I am the happiest I've ever been in my entire life! But, Lord, I want Your will to be done. I will accept whatever plan You have for me."

The next morning, I told Tim about my fears. He felt my stomach and admitted that he too could feel the lump. We cried and prayed together. Then he called several friends and arranged an appointment for me to see an oncologist, the best in the Chicago area, that very morning. I called my former oncologist to have my medical records faxed to the new physician's office.

Tim cancelled his day of work to take me to the doctor. When the nurse called me into the examination room, I cast a lingering glance at Tim, took a deep breath, and followed her from the waiting area. After putting on a gown and giving the nurse a urine sample, I waited for what seemed like hours for the doctor to appear. I liked him immediately. His gentle smile and kind manner put me at ease. I lay down on the examination table while he palpated my abdomen. His face looked grim as he studied my medical records.

"Yes, I can feel the lump." He indicated for me to sit up on the edge of the table.

"I need more tests before I can give you a diagnosis, but I want to send you to another doctor who specializes in uterine and ovarian cancer." He gave me the name and number of a gynecological oncologist. Turning to face the far wall, he resumed reading my records while I waited and prayed.

After a few minutes the office nurse returned to the examination room and asked the doctor if she could speak with him for a moment. They stepped out into the hallway. I strained to hear what they were saying. The only voice I heard was that of the doctor's.

"That's not possible! Run it again!"

A few minutes later the doctor returned and asked me to lie down on the table again. "I want to check one more thing." He turned toward his nurse. "Please hand me a Doppler." Being a nurse, I knew what a Doppler was. I'd used it many times in the emergency room to hear the fetal heartbeat of a pregnant patient. But I'd never seen it used for tumors. He moved the instrument around here and there and then held it in one place and chuckled.

"Well, this tumor has a heartbeat!"

What was he talking about? Was this some kind of secret code he shared with his nurse when he discovered something serious? The doctor glanced my way and could see the confusion on my face.

He grinned again. "Ma'am, you're not going to die! You're going to have a baby!"

"What? That's impossible! I've had radiation. I'm supposed to be sterile!"

He shook his head. "I don't have the answers. I can't believe it's possible. I didn't even ask my nurse to run a pregnancy test. She did it out of habit. When she first told me, I had her run it again." Twice the test had come back positive. Turning up the volume on the Doppler machine, he let me hear my baby's heartbeat. "Can you hear it?"

"Yes! Yes, I can." Tears that had welled up in my eyes now spilled over and trickled down the sides of my face onto the pillow beneath my head. Uncontrollable sobs spilled out from me as well. The nurse came over and hugged me. Realizing that I still clutched the name and phone number of the oncologist in my hand, I handed it to the doctor. "I-I-I guess I won't need this."

"I guess not." He handed me a tissue.

I couldn't stop crying. "I can't believe it. I walked in here fearing the worst, and I'm walking out carrying a gift from God."

The physician shook his head. "I'm really not a church-going man, but I'd have to say that if there is a God, He must have had something to do with this!"

CHAPTER 14

Surprise! Surprise!

My fingers didn't want to work correctly as I fumbled to do up the buttons on my blouse. Tim was still out in the waiting room, pacing the floor, anxious to hear the results. I had to hurry to give him the good news. Finally I stepped through the door into the crowded waiting room.

"Tim—"

"Oh, honey!" Seeing my tear-stained face he automatically assumed the worst. Bounding across the room, he swept me into his arms and buried my face in his shoulder.

"The doctor says . . ." I hiccoughed through a sob.

"Look, I don't care what the doctor says, we are going to fight this thing, do you hear me? We are going to fight it!"

My tears continued to roll. "But, Tim, the doctor told me—"

"It doesn't matter what he told you. I don't care how many doctors we need to go to, I'm not giving up on you!"

"Tim, stop! Please stop! It's not what you think."

With his hands on my upper arms, he stepped back and searched my face for answers. I giggled through my tears.

"Tim, I'm not going to die. We're going to have a baby!"

"Huh?" He froze for several seconds and then swept me off my feet and swung me in circles. "A baby?"

"Yes!"

"Are you sure you're not going to die?"

"Yes."

"A baby?"

I nodded enthusiastically.

Tim and Brenda eagerly awaiting the birth of their "miracle baby."

"Really?"

"Yes! Yes!" By now we were both laughing and crying at the same time, oblivious to those around us. Suddenly we became aware of enthusiastic applause coming from the other people in the waiting area. Many were crying as well.

We hurried home to tell Becky that she was going to have a baby brother or sister.

"Really?"

"That's right, honey."

"The baby's a girl, Mommy." Her eyes twinkled with delight.

"Well, honey, it could be a boy as well," I reminded her.

"No! It's a girl. When I prayed, God brought me Daddy. And I've been praying for a sister, so I know the baby's a girl." In her mind there was no doubt.

With Tim's promotion and planning for the move to San Jose, California, the next few days were busy and filled with mixed feelings on my part. My primary desire was to support Tim and his career, but I also had a longing to be close to my family at such an important time in our lives with the expectation of a new baby.

The move across country went smoothly. We settled into a lovely four-bedroom home with a large family room that doubled as a playroom for Becky. What I loved most about our new home were the fruit trees in the fenced-in backyard—two orange trees, a fig, a pomegranate, an apricot, a cherry, and a lemon tree, to name a few. Becky loved living next to the clubhouse, which had three Olympic-sized swimming pools. While I fixed supper each evening, Tim would return from work and take Becky swimming. The hour before dinner became their bonding time. In addition to the swimming, he would help her with her homework and listen to her stories of the day's events. Watching

Tim and Becky play "kitty cat" on the living-room floor warmed my heart. If only Tim's business associates could see him crawling around on all fours and meowing like a cat. That would certainly make them chuckle!

We had been living in California for a couple of months when Tim came home unexpectedly during the day. He'd forgotten some important papers and came home to retrieve them. Becky was at school, and I'd been mopping the kitchen floor. With the music playing, I didn't hear him open the front door and call my name.

Suddenly I saw a movement behind me. I saw a man standing in the doorway. Startled I threw down the mop and scrambled under the table for cover. This response was automatic because of the abuse I'd received while married to Dave. Shaking with fear, I covered my head with my hands and waited for the first blow that I knew would come at any second. At that moment in my mind Dave was back and the nightmare had started all over again. I wasn't able to rationally consider that this could not possibly be happening since I was now married to a kind and gentle man. I felt the man grasp my arm and pull me out from under the table. By now I was crying and pleading with him not to hurt me.

I felt my body being pulled across the tile floor. I braced myself for what I was convinced would come. But instead of a punch or a kick, Tim gently pulled me to him and hugged me tightly. Gasping for breath, I looked into his face and suddenly came to my senses. It was Tim!

Tim's face was wracked with a devastated look, and he was crying. "Honey, I would never hit you, don't you know that?" He ran his fingers through my hair. "I could never hurt you! I love you so much!" Tears rolled down his cheeks. "How could you possibly think for one minute that I would ever lay a hand on you? I swore before God to protect you, not hurt you. I would lay down my life for you."

I was so distraught I couldn't speak.

"No one will ever hurt you again! No one! Not ever!"

Tim was so unnerved by what happened that day he vowed that during disagreements he would never even raise his voice to me. He also determined never to startle me again.

One night as I put Becky down for the night, Tim said he wanted to talk to me about something important. As soon as she'd fallen asleep, I found him studying in his office. I paused in the doorway and, for a moment, watched him poring over a stack of papers. Suddenly he looked up and smiled.

"What is it, honey?" I asked.

He reached down and pulled an official-looking envelope from his briefcase. "It's the adoption papers. I've been talking with an attorney about starting the adoption proceedings for Becky."

"Wonderful." I glided into the room and made myself comfortable in the giant mahogany leather club chair beside his desk.

"Not really." He eyed me carefully. "I was told that I could not adopt her without her biological father's consent." He took a deep breath. "So our attorney drew up consent forms and mailed them to Dave."

"Yes, and . . ."

He handed the envelope to me. "What you're holding is his answer! He says he will never consent and that when Becky is ten he will start visitation."

Shocked, I fell back against the chair. In five years Dave had never so much as sent a birthday card. Becky had never seen him, didn't have any idea of what he looked like. He'd never attempted to call her or to see her—ever! Why would he want to visit her when she reached ten? She'd be scared to death of him. And so would I!

Tears welled up in my eyes. Tim came over, drew me from the chair, and held me in his arms. We stood for some time physically supporting one another. Tim spoke first.

"We should pray about it. Maybe God will soften Dave's heart and he'll change his mind."

I had wanted us to be a real family—legally. But now I felt this desire even more strongly. The very thought of this evil man disrupting our lives by visiting Becky even for a short time made me shudder. What might he do to her if he had one of his outbursts?

"Tim, I can't let this happen! I can't! It's more than I can bear."

"I know, I know." He rubbed my back gently, calming me down.

The next morning after Tim left for work and Becky left for school, I sat down at our kitchen table to have my morning worship. But all I could think of was Dave marching into my life again and tearing our world apart.

"Oh, dear God, someone must soften his heart." I knew Dave's heart more than anyone. I knew it would take a miracle for that to happen. But I also knew God never forced Himself on anyone. He can't soften a heart that has been hardened against Him.

"Father, show me what to do!"

Several hours later I got an idea. At first the very thought of it terrified me. The more I considered it, the more convinced I became that this was what I must do. After making a few phone calls to Kentucky to some friends who knew Dave, I accumulated some valuable information. First I learned the name of Dave's supervisor and the addresses and phone numbers of where he worked and lived. I also discovered that he had not only fathered Michelle from his first marriage, and Becky, but he also had a daughter by the woman who called me during our marriage. Since I had left, he'd married twice more and had two more daughters, one from each of those marriages. Knowing Dave as I did, I was quite sure he would not want to add Becky's name to his list of child support payments.

Since it was Friday, I decided to take the weekend to pray and ask God for guidance and wisdom. I agonized all weekend and could think of little else. On Sunday Tim and Becky spent the day at the pool and didn't notice that I was distracted.

Once the house was quiet on Monday morning, I was convinced that I had to follow through on my plan. I made the call to Dave. I chose to call him at work to avoid speaking with his newest wife. My hand trembled as I dialed the number. I almost changed my mind when the disinterested voice of the police dispatcher came on the line. I asked to speak with Dave Logan and was put on hold for what seemed like forever.

"Hello, Dave Logan here!" It was amazing how after five years his voice still made me quake in fear. I couldn't show fear in my voice. Too much was at stake. I swallowed hard. "Hello?" he asked again.

"Hello, Dave, this is Brenda."

It was as if the recording had never stopped. I cringed at the obscenities. "Well, what the ——are you calling me at work for? Let me tell you right now that if you're calling about those paternity papers, I am not signing them! Not now; not ever!" His fury exploded through the phone lines. "I already told your———lawyer that! So you can just go to———!"

"Yes, I know." I managed to maintain a much calmer voice than I felt inside. In a firm, authoritative tone which even surprised me, I said, "Before you say anything more, I want you to just listen to me. You have not paid child support for five years!"

"You———!"

I shouted into the telephone. "I told you to shut up and listen! Do not interrupt me again!" I had never raised my voice to him. He was probably too stunned to know what to say. "As I was saying, you have not paid child support in five years. My attorney tells me that in child support alone, you owe me $150 a month for five years which totals $9,000—that is not counting all the medical bills. Becky's been in and out of the hospital frequently, which totals to well over $100,000. My attorney also tells me that I am entitled to cost-of-living increases over the last five years, which I would have no trouble getting in court. All in all, I figure that you owe me somewhere around $150,000, give or take a few."

The rage building inside of him exploded. "Why you———!"

I cut him off before he could say more. Raising my voice even louder than his, I shouted, "I haven't told you the best part! You'd better listen good for this one! I suggest you think long and hard before you decide not to sign those paternity papers because it will cost you a lot more than money."

"What the———are you talking about?"

"I'm talking about your job! You are a police officer, and when you took the job you took an oath to uphold the law. Well, guess what, buddy! It is against the law not to pay child support, so you will be fired! You can't be a policeman and break the law! You will lose your job! You're going to have a hard time paying me the $150,000 that I'll take from you when you're out of work." By now I was wound up. "You may even do jail time. I hear they're hard on ex-cops in prison."

I took a deep breath. "And, oh, just in case you think I'm bluffing, I want you to know that I have your supervisor's name and number—Bill

Foster, right? I have his home phone number too. Let's see. Today is Monday. If my attorney does not have the paternity papers signed by you and on his desk by Friday, I have instructed him to file papers against you. Believe me when I say, I am not kidding! Sergeant Foster will hear from me. It's your choice; you decide!"

Click! I hung up the phone before he could reply. I hugged myself to control the trembling that coursed through my body. I sank down in my chair, completely drained! I couldn't believe I had actually stood up to the man who had controlled me for so long. I meant every word of what I said. There was no reason to feel guilty, as he had made me feel in the past.

Knowing Tim didn't want me to have any contact with Dave and knowing that if Tim had called Dave he would have only made my ex-husband angrier, I kept it between God and me. Now all I could do was wait.

I didn't have to wait long. Around eleven o'clock the next morning our attorney called.

"You are not going to believe what just arrived by Federal Express!"

My heart began thumping wildly in my chest. A huge smile spread across my face. I knew exactly what he was about to tell me.

"I just received the paternity papers from your ex-husband, and they are signed! There is no explanation, just the signed papers. We can go ahead with the adoption. I'll finish the rest of the paperwork, get a court date, and get back to you."

Ecstatic, I jumped up and down, twirled in circles, and praised God. Now I would never again have to worry about Dave interfering in Becky's life. He could no longer take her from me. He could not hurt her as he had me so many times during our marriage. My daughter would never feel the wrath of one of his outbursts. The nightmare was over. She was safe! And I, too, was finally totally free of him.

A few weeks later our little family met in the judge's chambers. The judge indicated that we should sit down. I was very nervous. Becky immediately jumped into Tim's lap. The judge looked at Tim.

"Are you prepared to be a father for Becky? Do you understand that once you sign these papers you become responsible for her in every way for the rest of her life?"

Tim nodded. "I love this little girl very much. She has filled my heart with more love than I'd have ever thought possible. I love Brenda and Becky with all my heart, and I want the three of us to be a real family."

The judge glanced over the rim of his glasses at me and my expanding belly. "Don't you mean the four of you?"

We laughed together.

"You know, sir, my life was empty before I met Becky and my wife. Now I feel like the richest man in the world."

The judge's eyes watered; his face softened further. "And how about you, little lady? Do you want this man to be your daddy?"

Becky gave Tim a protective hug. "This is my daddy, and I love him. Even if you don't sign the papers, he will still be my daddy!"

The judge threw back his head and laughed. "Well, that's good enough for me." He removed his pen from the holder, signed the papers and handed them to Tim. "Congratulations, Dad!" And then he turned to Becky, "Young lady, you are now officially Rebecca Lynn Walsh." His voice broke. We were all on the verge of weeping.

Before we left his chambers, the judge shook hands with each of us. When he bent to shake Becky's hand he said, "It's days like this that make me glad to be a judge."

We left his office hand in hand, legally and otherwise a real family.

A couple of weeks before the baby was due, Tim heard that he had an important business meeting in Florida at the same time. His manager, while sympathetic, was adamant. "Baby or no baby, you must be at that meeting!"

At my prenatal visit that week I talked with my doctor to see if he thought the baby would be coming soon. I shared with him Tim's dilemma and how much I wanted Tim to be there for the birth. Though I showed no signs that delivery was near, my obstetrician suggested he induce labor.

So on February 26 Tim and I went to the hospital while my sister Linda, who had flown in to help me with the new baby, cared for Becky. By noon, I'd made no progress. By five in the afternoon I was still dilated only two centimeters. The doctor wanted to send me home. I begged to be allowed to try a little longer.

Contractions came and went. The pain was unbelievable. Poor Tim's back ached from leaning over the bed, and his hand had lost all feeling from my squeezing it so hard during the contractions. I knew he was trying to help, but I was desperate. In the middle of the worst contraction I yelled at him. "Stop telling me to breathe!"

Eager to please, he responded, "OK, honey, don't breathe! Don't breathe!"

After sixteen hours of hard labor, Linda Kay Walsh was born, weighing seven pounds, thirteen ounces. She was perfect, with long black hair, blue eyes, and the cut-

Brenda and Linda Kay, five days old.

est little nose. Best of all, despite the radiation therapy I'd had, she was perfectly healthy. Praise the Lord, for He is good!

CHAPTER 15

Evidence of God's Care

When Linda Kay was three years old, Tim was promoted to corporate headquarters at Digital Equipment Corporation near Boston, Massachusetts. I dreaded leaving California's great weather and our friends. I knew that I would miss both terribly. Saying goodbye to my friend Sally and my neighbor Mecca hurt, but the anticipation of decorating the new home we were having built in Groton sweetened the move for me.

Anyone who has ever relocated across country understands the exhaustion that comes as a result. Packing up the family belongings is long, hard work, and moving into the new place takes major organization. Even with Tim's employer hiring a moving company to do all the packing, loading, and unloading, someone must stand in the entryway of the new place and direct traffic. Tim tried, but like it or not, that someone ended up being me, despite the fact that I was doubled over with pain.

I had been awake the previous night with a persistent dull pain in my stomach. By noon on move-in day I could barely stand upright enough to tell the movers into which room to place specific boxes and pieces of furniture. Tim kept asking me throughout the morning if I was OK and insisting that I rest. But I kept pressing on, assuring him I would make it.

After the last box had been deposited in the appropriate location, Tim rushed me to the closest emergency room. A medical team examined me, drew vials of blood, and took X-rays and an ultrasound. Hours later they admitted me. Tim and I waited anxiously to speak with the

attending specialist. When he
arrived and studied my chart,
he looked grim.

"Mrs. Walsh, we've spotted
a tumor on one of your ovaries.
We need to schedule you for
surgery right away."

My breath caught in my
throat. *Oh, no!* I'd been through
this before. The year after
Linda Kay's birth, my gyne-
cologist in California had
warned me that I had a precancerous growth on my uterus. "If
you don't have a hysterectomy
soon it could cost you your
life."

I wanted more children, but

Tim playing with his daughters

Tim didn't hesitate. "I don't want to lose you for anything. You have to have
the hysterectomy." And so I did. However, at that time my ovaries showed
no sign of cancer. Because of my young age, the doctors left them intact.

And now I faced another cancer surgery.

I stared at the tile on the floor while the doctor continued. "The
ultrasound revealed a tumor the size of a walnut on your right ovary."

I'd worked as a surgical nurse for two years, so I could visualize the
entire procedure. I knew surgery was a must, but what about the scar-
ring? I asked, "What type of scar will I have?"

"Excuse me?" The doctor seemed surprised by my question.

"Would you please give me a Pfannenstiel incision?"

"A bikini incision?" His eyes softened, and a smile teased at the corners of his lips.

"Yes, with a subcuticular stitch." I grinned.

He broke into laughter. "Only a nurse would be so picky! We'll see
what we can do."

On the day of my surgery, just so the doctor wouldn't forget, I drew a
dotted line with a thin Magic Marker in the location where I wanted the

incision to go. Above the dotted line I wrote, "Please cut along dotted line." I knew that the operating-room personnel would get a good laugh out of my message to the surgeon.

When I awoke from surgery the nurse explained that my right ovary had been removed as it had signs of precancerous growth, but they had left my left ovary in place, again because of my age.

I quietly took in the information. I thanked God silently for sparing my life once again. I was also grateful that I would have one ovary so I wouldn't need hormone replacement therapy. Most of all I was grateful that I would be alive to watch my children grow.

"What about my bikini line?"

She grinned and then helped me lift my head enough to see my abdomen.

Written in bright red marker across my stomach was, "For services rendered, $3,000.00," signed by my surgeon. I could not control my laughter, which brought on more pain and the need for an additional dose of pain medication.

The next day the floor nurse had just given me Dilaudid IV for pain before leaving for her lunch break. In a hurry, she didn't chart it immediately as she should have done. She figured she would do so upon her return. Five minutes later her replacement entered my room and checked my chart. There was no record of pain medication being given me in four hours. Since I was already drowsy from the first shot, I couldn't tell her I'd already had one dose. So she gave me a second shot of Dilaudid IV.

The second dose depressed my respiration so much that I was hardly breathing. Any medication given intravenously is absorbed into the body much faster than it would be when given in pill form.

In God's perfect timing, Tim and the girls came to visit a few minutes later, along with his brother Bill, who'd flown in to see me as well. As Tim approached my bedside he noticed that my color looked almost white and my lips were blue. He bent down to kiss me and could barely feel my breath.

He dashed to the nurse's station. "Quick, my wife is barely breathing!"

The floor nurse smiled indulgently. "Mr. Walsh, I'm sure she's fine. I was just in there checking on her."

Tim rushed back to my bedside. By this time I'd stopped breathing entirely. Not caring who heard him, he shouted down the hallway, "She's stopped breathing! Do something! My wife isn't breathing!"

Immediately the woman came running. She called a "code blue," the hospital terminology for a patient needing CPR. A swarm of hospital personnel rushed into the room while the floor nurse shouted orders. Our terrified daughters began crying hysterically.

"Get those children out of here!" the nurse shouted as she hauled the dividing curtain around my bed. Tim's brother hurried our two daughters from the room. "You go too, Mr. Walsh!"

"No! I'm staying right here!"

Not having time to argue, she returned her attention to my condition. Tim watched as they performed CPR on me, praying that God would spare my life. After several minutes the heart monitor began beeping once again. Taking a deep breath, he ran a frazzled hand through his hair. "Oh, dear God, thank You! Thank You for giving me back my wife!"

Later, when the narcotics had worn off and I could understand what had happened, I was horrified. It was unnerving to think how fast I could have slipped away with no goodbyes, no last-minute anything! I had no doubt that God had a purpose for my life—a special plan. What it might be, I had no idea.

I thought about all the times in my life that God had spared me from certain death. As a toddler when I fell from a moving car; the many times in my first marriage when I was left for dead; several snowstorms where I should have frozen to death; and countless other times. *"Lord, You keep saving me. Why? What do You have planned for me?"*

Three months later I experienced the same kind of pain again. This time I knew exactly what it was—a tumor on my left ovary. My doctor confirmed it and scheduled another surgery for me. As I lay on the gurney in the operating room, my surgeon asked if I had any surprise this time.

"I guess you'll just have to check and see." I cast him a mischievous smile.

He laughed. The nurse pulled back the sheet. And resting on my last incision site was a bright purple zipper with the words written above it, "Why not just put in a zipper this time?"

A sense of humor helps during times of stress, but surgery is still surgery—a very serious undertaking. Yet as fearful as I was to undergo surgery again, I was terrified of post-op care since I had come close to dying the last time. To ease my fears, Tim arranged for my mother to fly east from Michigan to help care for me. She and Tim took turns staying with me and with the girls. Every medication given, they questioned. In addition the doctor wrote that no pain medication should be given unless I asked for it. This time recovery went smoothly.

Before I left the hospital to return home the doctor said, "You are not out of the woods yet. There is a fifty-fifty chance that the cancer could return. If you make it for five years cancer-free, we will consider you cured." The cancer has never returned. God spared my life again.

Marie, a new friend I'd made at church, helped care for me after my mother returned home. Two weeks after the surgery I was still experiencing complications and not allowed to drive, but I needed some groceries and things. Whenever I sent Tim to the grocery store, it seemed he came home with everything but what I had on the list. To get what I wanted, I needed to write down each item including size and brand.

Determined to do my own shopping, I asked Marie to take the girls and me to the store. I'd heard about a new supermarket nearby that had wonderful produce. She agreed. Marie, being a more practical person, came dressed in long shorts, casual shoes, and a practical top. As for me, I'd been bedridden for so long, I dressed in my best, right down to high heels.

I'd barely gotten down two aisles before I felt a grabbing pain near my incision site. I pressed my arm against my stomach and continued down the aisle. By the end of the aisle, I noticed the floor was moving beneath my feet. I staggered.

Thinking quickly, Marie took one look at me and sat me down on a large carton of toilet paper that had not yet been stacked on the shelves. "You sit here!" she said.

She grabbed my shopping list and started calling out orders. "Gena, you get the oats. Joli, you and Linda Kay get the flour and baking soda.

Becky, you get the olive oil." When one of the girls returned she'd send them on another assignment until the cart contained all the items on my list. The girls made a game of it, running through the store for food items and seeing who could return to the cart first.

In order to go to the checkout counter, I had to relinquish my toilet paper throne. Marie steadied me by the arm as I carefully took a few steps. I felt wobbly. She looked down at my high heels and shook her head.

"Here! Wear mine!" She traded shoes with me right in the middle of the aisle. We looked ridiculous, her wearing shorts and my dressy high heels; me in a fancy dress wearing her casual flats, but it worked.

Brenda's friend Marie, second from left, with her husband, Frank, and Tim and Brenda.

When we had the groceries checked out and bagged, I took out my checkbook and started to write.

"I'm sorry, ma'am, but we don't accept checks at this store. It is cash only." She pointed to a large sign on the wall.

Since I'd never shopped there before, I'd never noticed the sign on the wall.

"But I don't have any cash with me. You know it will cost the company an inordinate amount of time and money putting all these groceries back on their shelves. Couldn't you make an exception just this once?" I pleaded.

"Absolutely not!" She set her jaw and glared.

"May I speak with your manager, please?"

The manager was a tough older lady who had heard the entire exchange between the checkout woman and me, but she didn't care. "I'm sorry, there are no exceptions. It is cash only."

"All right, I guess I'll have to go elsewhere." I turned and headed for the door. Marie stared after me in total disbelief. We'd spent an hour and a half collecting all our groceries and now were having to leave them behind. With a shrug she followed me out of the store.

"Let's go to Shaw's," I suggested. "They take checks."

At Shaw's, my regular market, we did it all again, only this time it was much faster because we'd already gone through a dress rehearsal. To this day Marie and I remain close friends. Whenever we exchange gifts, there's always at least one gift that has something to do with shoes. Just thinking about our shoe exchange in the food market gives us a good laugh.

* * *

Tim and I had been living in New England for about a year when one day I received a call from Grammy. Even after my breakup with Jim, she and I had never lost contact. We loved each other so much that she welcomed Tim into her heart too. The first time she met him, she gave him a hug and told him that if I loved him, then she did too. After the death of Jim's father, Grammy remarried. And it was just like old times. Our friendship had begun before Jim and lasted beyond Jim. The night of our first visit to her home and long after the husbands went to bed, Grammy and I stayed up talking into the wee hours of the morning. Our special bond allowed me to tell her anything.

On this day, Grammy's voice on the phone was weak and shaky, and I knew something was wrong. "Brenda, is there any way you could come to Texas to see me?"

"What's wrong, Grammy? What the matter?"

She didn't speak for a second. "Hon, I'm in the hospital. I have cancer, and the doctors say I'm not going to make it. I would love to see you one more time before I go. Do you think you could come?"

By now I was in tears. This precious lady was not one to exaggerate or make things up. "Oh, Grammy, please don't say that. Surely there is something the doctors can do. Please don't give up!"

"Brenda, don't cry. I'm ready to go. I know that the next voice I hear will be the voice of Jesus. I'm not afraid."

"Grammy!"

"Brenda, I want you to know that even though you did not marry my son, you have been my daughter in every way. I couldn't love you more if you were my own flesh and blood."

"I know, Grammy. I know. I love you too with all my heart." What a nightmare—losing Grammy. This just couldn't happen! I had to catch my breath. "I'll come right away."

She ended with, "Hurry, Hon, I don't know how much time I have left."

Seconds later I was on the phone to Tim and he was encouraging me to go. "Don't worry about the girls. We'll manage. You just pack, and I'll make the flight arrangements." When I hung up from talking with Tim, I called my old friend Susan and asked her to meet my plane in Dallas. She agreed.

On the way to the airport Tim glanced across the car at me. "You know, Brenda, Jim will probably be there."

I started at the thought. All I could think of was losing Grammy and how much I wanted to see her before she died. Seeing Jim again hadn't crossed my mind.

He continued. "You and Jim never really had any closure. I interrupted that the night we met. If you want to go out to dinner to talk things out, it's OK with me. For that matter, I think it would be good."

"Tim, I haven't even thought along those lines."

"I know. But I want you to know that I'm fine with it. I know you love me and it's OK. I think it would be good for both of you."

My eyes misted as I reached across the car and placed my hand on his thigh. *Lord, how I love this man You gave me.*

The plane ride from Boston to Dallas seemed to take forever. My mind bounced from one memory to the next. I recalled the time Grammy had shown up at my little house in Dallas when I was in nursing school. I'd been sick with a 103-degree temperature. I knew if I took sick time, I wouldn't be able to graduate on time. I was struggling just to show up for classes, do my clinicals, study, and care for Becky. I didn't know how much longer I could carry on. An hour after I prayed to God for healing and help, Grammy showed up at my door unannounced. She stayed for two weeks, cleaning, cooking, and caring for

Becky so that I could study. She refused to leave until I was completely back to health.

I closed my eyes, and I could smell the wonderful aroma of her pineapple upside-down cake that she cooked in her Crock-Pot. I'd never heard of a cake cooking in a Crock-Pot, but Grammy made them, and they were absolutely delicious. Every time she knew I was coming for a visit she'd have one waiting for me. I just couldn't imagine my life without my precious Grammy.

I remembered the weekends Becky and I spent on her farm, especially the day I spotted a huge rattlesnake in the garden. Following my blood-curdling scream, Grammy came running.

"Don't move!" She grabbed a nearby hoe and, with one mighty whack, ended the rattler's life. I was shaking all over, but she just laughed. "That happens all the time. You're in Texas, honey!"

The plane landed. I gathered my belongings and made my way into the air terminal. I gazed about the crowd and spotted Susan waving toward me. She'd been crying.

"Susan, what's wrong?"

She couldn't talk at first.

"What's happened? Is it Grammy?"

She nodded. "Oh Brenda, I don't know how to tell you this, but Grammy died twenty minutes ago. I just made a call from the pay phone while I was waiting for you. I can't believe it! I am so sorry."

"No! No! That's not possible!" *How could I have missed her by just twenty minutes? Oh, God, why couldn't she have waited just one hour longer?* Crying hysterically, I collapsed into the nearest chair. Susan put her arms around me, and we cried together.

After I composed myself and retrieved my luggage, we drove to Susan's house. No longer was there a need to hurry to the hospital. I was numb with shock and disappointment. I couldn't stop crying.

"At least she knew you were on your way to her," Susan said. "And she knew how much you loved her."

Susan had learned from the family that there would be a viewing the next evening. I could wait until then to pay my respects. That night I shared my memories of Grammy with Susan, and she held me while I cried.

The next afternoon I asked Susan to take me to the funeral home a little before the scheduled time for the viewing. I wanted a few minutes alone with her before everyone else arrived. Susan understood. She waited in the lobby while I walked into the room where Grammy's casket rested.

I'd never expected to see my beloved Grammy in a casket. My grandfather was the only close family member who had died in my life, and I'd not been able to attend his funeral. Often I'd been hired to play the organ at viewings and funerals. I could never understand why family members would touch the body. Now it didn't seen strange to me at all. I picked up one of Grammy's cold, stiff hands and began to talk with her, as if she were there in the room. I knew she couldn't hear me, but somehow it helped to talk to her anyway. I told her how much I loved her and how much I would treasure forever all the wonderful memories I had of her.

Grammy didn't look like herself. Her skin was scaly and red. Hours before she died, she'd had an allergic reaction to a medication she'd been given. If the medication hadn't taken her life, the cancer would have. But if it weren't for the medication, I would have been able to tell her goodbye in person. This made me cry harder.

Deep in my own grief, I don't know how long I stayed in the room before I sensed someone come up behind me and put his arms around me. Instantly I knew it was Jim. We stood in silence for several minutes. He was desperately trying to contain his emotion. Finally he leaned down and whispered in my ear, "Now I have lost you both." With a gentle squeeze he left the room as silently as he'd arrived.

Overcome with emotion, I leaned over the casket and laid my head across Grammy's arms—those same loving arms that had held me so many times before. I felt two hands on my shoulders. It was Susan. "Come on, Brenda. Let's go back to the house."

CHAPTER 16

Life Goes On

When the telephone rang that evening, I sensed it was Jim. Susan answered it and, with a wary eye, handed the receiver to me.

"Hello? Jim? How are you doing?"

"I could be better, but that's not why I'm calling. I was wondering if you would be willing to play the organ at the funeral tomorrow. Grammy always loved it when you played for her."

I'd played at hundreds of funerals over the years. I even played at Oscar's funeral; but Grammy's? "Jim," I said, "I loved Grammy so much, I wish I could do this for her, but I just can't. I'd never make it through. Please apologize to your family for me. I truly am sorry."

"It's all right. I understand. Would you consider sitting beside me during the funeral? It would mean a lot to me."

I took a deep breath and swallowed hard. "Jim, I'd like to be there for emotional support. But considering we dated for four years, it wouldn't be appropriate for me to be by your side. Everyone knows I'm a married woman, and since Tim couldn't be here, I'm afraid it would send the wrong message. I hope you understand." I knew Jim was disappointed.

"Yes, I guess I do. OK, then, I'll see you tomorrow." He said Goodbye and hung up the phone.

I immediately called Tim and told him everything that had happened. His love reached out to me over the phone and comforted me.

"Honey, I love you, and I am praying for you."

The next morning the church was packed with people, reminding me that Grammy had touched many people's lives. I watched the family file in and take their places in the front rows. As Jim passed by I avoided looking directly at him for fear our eyes would meet and I would lose what little composure I still had. The minister said wonderful things about Grammy, but they paled in comparison to the woman I knew. How sad life would be without her!

Having Susan by my side for support was a comfort, and I thanked God for her friendship. Whenever I started to weep she would put her arm around me or take my hand. At the end of the funeral the family formed a receiving line at the back of the church. The idea of greeting each of these people, who'd believed that one day I would be part of their family, was too much to bear. I paused to pray for courage.

"Let's slip out the side door," Susan said, pointing to an exit from the sanctuary. We crossed the parking lot to her car. I'd just closed my door when I heard a tap on the window. It was Jim peering in at me. He gestured for me to roll down the window.

"Are you going to the cemetery?" He looked hopeful.

"No, I'm sorry, but I can't go through that." I'd sung at the grave sites of many people with no problem, but not Grammy's. I just couldn't.

"I understand." He leaned forward. "Brenda, would it be possible to take you to dinner tomorrow night? I really would love the chance to talk to you, to clear something up."

As I gazed up into Jim's pleading eyes I remembered my husband's admonition. "Go to dinner with him. You both need closure."

I nodded.

A weak smile spread across his face. "Great. I'll call you about the time."

The old phrase "living on pins and needles" aptly described my feelings throughout the next day. Part of me wanted to run away; the other part eagerly anticipated the chance to understand what had happened between us.

Jim picked me up at Susan's. It was awkward. In the car, we talked about the funeral, the beautiful bouquets of flowers, the pastor's kind words, and the people who had attended. He recounted for me the graveside ceremony. He managed to stretch his observations until we reached the restaurant. The maitre d' guided us to a table, and we sat down.

I browsed the menu—enchiladas, chile relleno, vegetable fajitas, sopapillas—all my favorites. "Everything looks so good!"

Jim smiled across the table at me. "Um, I remembered how much you enjoyed Mexican food."

"It's been so long since I've had a good chile relleno! Since we moved from California, in fact! Do you know how difficult it is to get authentic Mexican food in Massachusetts?" We both gave a nervous laugh.

We were relieved when the waiter arrived to take our order. He also took the menus, a kind of protective barrier we'd erected between us. Jim leaned back.

"So, tell me about Tim."

"Yes, there is so much I want to tell you about him. He is such a thoughtful and loving man and so good to me. As you know, he works for . . ." I went on for some time, nervously nibbling on tortilla chips and lauding my husband's accomplishments.

"Your girls—you have another besides Becky, right?"

"Yes, Linda Kay. What can I say about the lights of my life? They are such beautiful little ladies. Becky is ten going on twenty."

He chuckled.

"And Linda Kay? What a miracle baby!"

Before I could catch my breath, he asked, "And your parents?"

"Oh, you know my folks—never a dull moment. Dad is pastoring two churches in Michigan. And Mom is working right beside him. In fact Dad is preparing for a series of evangelistic meetings." Again I waxed eloquent, describing their busy lives. I told him where each of my siblings was living and what they were doing. He asked about my job at the hospital.

"I'm still working in the emergency room. You know how much I love it. Why just the other day—"

"Brenda, how could you possibly think I didn't love Becky?"

My mouth dropped open. Talk about getting right to the point! His voice thickened with emotion as he continued.

"I loved Becky so much! She was so adorable and sweet and a duplicate of you! I would have had to be made out of stone not to have loved her."

"But you told me that you didn't want her to call you Daddy. I felt that you would never let her get close to you. I thought you didn't want to be a father to her!" Choked with emotion, I could barely talk.

His eyes glistened with tears. "It was precisely because I did love her that I would not let her call me Daddy. You wouldn't commit to marrying me and let me be her daddy. Every time I asked, you put me off." His intense gaze bored through me. "You are the only woman I have ever asked to marry me. I wanted to spend the rest of my life with you. But after all you'd been through, I wasn't sure you would ever agree to marry me or anyone else for that matter."

Stunned, I could barely catch my breath.

"Brenda, I loved Becky so much that I didn't want her to get emotionally attached to me only to have you leave me and break her heart. I'd decided that until you were able to commit to me, I had to keep her at a distance . . . for her sake."

By now we were both weeping, overwrought with the years of useless pain. Our food came, but we didn't touch it. We sat there in silence, each of us struggling to regain our composure. I was the first to speak.

"Jim, I am so sorry. I should have told you how I felt. I should have trusted you enough to discuss my concerns with you." I drew circles in the moisture on the outside of my water glass. "Jim, there must be another reason why we are not together. I believe that God had other plans for our lives." I told him how Tim and I met and how God brought us together. I told him about my bouts with cancer and getting pregnant despite the radiation treatments. "Surely you can see God's hand in all of this."

He was quiet for a moment and then leaned across the table toward me. "I'll tell you what I believe. I believe that we were supposed to be together. I believe that Tim or anyone else could never love you the way I love you. And I believe you married Tim for the wrong reasons."

I sat up straight, intending to set him straight, but he continued. "I know that you cannot possibly share the kind of love with him that we shared with each other. I also know that, as a mother, you would sacrifice your own feelings for the future of your daughter."

"No, you have it all wrong—"

"I have no doubt that you have a love for Tim. I know you wouldn't marry anyone you didn't have some kind of love for, but he will never occupy the place in your heart that I have!"

"No, Jim! That's not true. I love Tim with all my heart. He's a wonderful husband. We have a beautiful life together."

By the closed look on his face I knew my protestations were useless. Yes, there should have been closure years before. Without it, Jim had fantasized a relationship with me that could never be. This came clear in his next comment.

"Nothing you say will ever convince me. Someday, when your children are grown, I know you will come back to me. We will be together. And I want you to know that I will wait for you as long as it takes!"

"Jim, I think you'd better take me back to Susan's place." My hands shook as I gathered up my purse to leave.

"Brenda, as long as it takes!" He reached across the table to place his hand on mine. Instantly, I removed my hand from his grasp.

As we said Goodbye outside Susan's home, I had no way of knowing it would be the last time I would see him. Two years later, in Pensacola, Florida, two teenagers who were drinking while driving hit Jim's car head-on. He died instantly. Jim was buried in Texas near his parents.

* * *

Jim was wrong about me. I loved being Tim's wife, and I was absolutely in love with him. He had become my best friend. At night, we often fell asleep talking about anything and everything. We would share the day's events concerning the girls. I would tell him about my day; he would tell me about his. Tim loved me and adored his "girls." He always put us first. He was a "hands-on" dad. While I fixed dinner each evening, he helped the girls with their homework—especially with their math and science assignments. I loved being a mother to my little girls and delighted in watching them so involved with their daddy. This was the Christian family I'd once believed was beyond my wildest dreams.

That's not to say there weren't challenges. A determined child from a young age, Linda Kay kept both of us on our "spiritual toes." One time I sent her to her room for misbehaving. After I instructed her to ask Jesus to forgive her for the way she'd been acting, she stomped up to her room. Just minutes later however, she bounded down the stairs. I looked up in surprise.

"Now you just wait one minute, Linda Kay—"

Before I could finish my admonition, she lifted her hand like a traffic cop. "Don't worry about it, Mom. Jesus and me worked it out."

I coughed and sputtered and left the room quickly to keep from allowing her to see me laugh.

Another time she'd been disciplined several times through the day. I was kneeling with her beside her bed, listening to her bedtime prayers.

"Now, Jesus, where were You today? I asked You this morning to help me be a good girl. So what happened? Don't leave me tomorrow, OK?"

I learned my homemaking skills from my mother, a pastor's wife. She taught me to keep an entrée and a dessert in the freezer at all times for last-minute guests. As a result, Tim could call from the office any morning and tell me he was bringing home several of his managers for dinner that evening and I'd be ready. Today he gives me and my hospitality skills credit for helping him climb the corporate ladder. I think it's my mom who really deserves the praise.

But most of all, I enjoyed having a Christian husband, one who went to church with me each week, who participated in the operation of the church. While he was busy with his responsibilities as deacon and chairman of the finance committee, I was church clerk, organist, pianist, head of the social committee, and a leader in the children's divisions. I loved my family, and I loved being active and involved in my local church, I believed I was doing all I could for Jesus. Yet something seemed to be missing. Looking back, I can see God's hand preparing me for a service beyond the walls of my local church.

At the time, Tim and I were living in Bolton, Massachusetts, near Boston. The girls were in grade school. Tim was vice president of a videoconference company, which allowed him to travel all over the world. In addition to being a wife and mother, I worked as an occupational health-care nurse for a large company. I was also running a dried-flower business—as well as helping my sister with a Christian bookmark ministry. Yet with all the church work and day-by-day witnessing I did with friends and business associates, something was still missing. When I thought about all my heavenly Father had done for me, I hungered to do something more for Him. I began to pray for God's direction.

It all started with Sabbath dinner at my parents' new home in Tennessee. Tim and I were visiting from Boston. Their guests that day—and my childhood friends—were Danny Shelton, president of Three Angels Broadcasting Network (3ABN), and his brother Tommy. Danny shared inspiring stories about people he'd met and witnessed to on airplanes.* He said that before he left home for the airport he would pray a very special prayer. " 'Lord, please sit me next to somebody with whom I can share my faith.' And every time, without fail, God does just that."

As I listened to his stories, I became more and more excited. I'd never thought of doing such a thing. I felt as though I was just going through life fooling myself that I was a wonderful Christian fulfilling my little tasks at church and in my community, when there was so much more I could be doing for God.

Tommy and Danny Shelton and Elder and Mrs. Micheff with Brenda.

Something clicked inside of me. Suddenly I knew I wasn't doing enough for my Lord. I wondered what would happen if I prayed that kind of prayer. What would happen if I got up every morning and prayed, "Lord, will You use me in a special way today?"

During our long drive home I thought about the stories Danny told and how many people he'd helped learn more about Jesus. I really wanted to be used like that. And just as his experience began with a prayer, I determined in my heart to plead with God to let me be a servant, not just in normal, everyday things but to be used by God in ways that were above and beyond.

I began each day with that prayer. I'd pray in the shower, "Lord, You know I want to serve You. Please let me witness to somebody today. Use me in a special way. Help me be a blessing to someone."

I prayed that prayer many times a day, but life went on as usual. After the first week, I took stock. I couldn't pinpoint anything that seemed like what Danny had experienced. I began to wonder if something was wrong. Why hadn't God used me?

I increased my prayer time. As I drove in my car, I'd pray, "God, please help me be a blessing to somebody." Yet I still didn't have one story that I could claim as an example of God using me in a special way. After two weeks I was discouraged. I couldn't figure out why He wasn't using me. "God, if You could just show me in a small way—just a little way, let me know You're using me, I'd really appreciate it, if that's not too selfish. But if it's too selfish, I withdraw the request and I apologize. I'll just try to work on having more faith."

From then on I went back to my morning prayer to make me a blessing in someone's life today. Several days went by. Tim left for work around seven one morning. I awakened with the desire to make a batch of cookies.

I found my favorite cookbooks in the pantry and spread them out on the counter. *Hmm, I haven't made gingersnaps in a long time.* I gathered together all the ingredients and made a batch of gingersnaps and placed them in the oven. While they baked, I returned to my cookbooks. *Oatmeal cookies! I haven't made oatmeal cookies in months!* Before I knew it, I'd made oatmeal cookies. Then I made date bars. Browsing my cookbooks again, there were so many cookies that looked good to me. Molasses cookies were next.

It's a good thing I had a well-stocked pantry. I was in the habit of baking and cooking so much that I purchased my ingredients in large bulk. My flour came in fifty-pound bags. Friends would tease that they wanted to be at our house during the time of trouble because there was so much food in our pantry! I had enough ingredients to bake all day. And that is just what I did. Before I knew it, the door opened and I heard my husband's voice.

"Honey, are we having a party?"

"Why do you ask?"

He gazed about the room. "Cookies?"

For the first time I looked about the kitchen and realized how many cookies I'd made. There were cookies everywhere. There were cookies on the table, cookies on every counter, cookies on the cooling rack beside my sink, cookies spread across my cook-top stove. I entered the pantry and found cookies covering every surface. I found cookies on top of my chest freezer, on the dining-room table, on the kitchen table. Every possible surface held batches and batches of cookies.

As I looked at my baking spree, I was embarrassed. I didn't know what had happened, but for twelve hours I had baked cookies. Not only would my husband think he'd married a crazy woman, but I seriously wondered if I'd "lost it." Tears welled up in my eyes.

"Um, I don't know."

He looked from one surface to the next. "What are you going to do with them?"

"I guess I'll put them in the freezer."

By the time I bagged all the cookies and put them in the freezer, it was stuffed with cookies. There wasn't room for anything else.

A couple of weeks later, on Sabbath morning, I came down to the pantry, removed all the bags of cookies from the freezer and set them on the pantry counter. I returned upstairs, showered, and dressed for church. After a nice church service we returned home for Sabbath dinner. I played the piano while my husband listened from the sofa as he always did on Sabbath afternoon.

About four-thirty I went to the pantry to get a glass of water from our water cooler and gasped in surprise at seeing the mountain of cookies stacked on the counter. *What is wrong with me? I am really losing it!* I didn't remember taking them out of the freezer. And I certainly didn't know why I'd do such a thing. I was not only foolish for baking the cookies in the first place but foolish enough to take them out of the freezer and leave them on the counter all day. *What am I going to do with all these cookies?* My mother had taught me that I shouldn't refreeze foods once they had thawed—so that wasn't an option!

"I know!" I spoke to the pantry's empty walls. "I'll take them to a soup kitchen."

---

*You can read Danny Shelton's stories in *Mending Broken People: The Miracle Stories of 3ABN* by Kay Kuzma (3ABN/Pacific Press, 2005).

Becoming Miss Brenda

When I was eighteen, I thought I wanted to be Miss Kentucky. Strange, isn't it, how titles make us feel important?

I'm sure I would have enjoyed the prestige and attention—as well as the money—I would have received if I had won the Miss Kentucky beauty pageant. But God had another title He wanted to give me when I had grown to trust Him enough that He could trust me. The title He chose is simply "Miss Brenda."

There's probably not another person in the world who would want that title, but I humbly cherish the honor of sharing Jesus with a worldwide television audience of "children" of all ages.

The job certainly wasn't something I was looking for. I was happy in my Massachusetts "pasture," taking care of Tim and my grown girls, and enjoying the financial benefits I received from juggling three prosperous jobs.

Later, as the Miss Brenda job became more than a full-time responsibility, and flying back and forth to 3ABN became a major expense for Tim and me, I wondered why we would leave our daughters—and now a grandchild—on the east coast and move to Knoxville, Tennessee, so that I could drive six hours one way to volunteer my time working harder and longer hours than I have ever worked in my life. And why would Tim consent to make this move so that his wife could be closer to her work when it meant he would have to drive seven hours in the opposite direction to his? It doesn't make much sense, does it?

But when you've been redeemed, and God calls, it makes all the sense in the world.

Make a joyful shout to the LORD, all you lands!
Serve the LORD with gladness;
Come before His presence with singing.
Know that the LORD, He is God;
It is He who has made us, and not we ourselves,
We are His people
and the sheep of His pasture.
—*Psalm 100:1–3 (NKJV)*

CHAPTER 17

From Cookie Lady to Miss Brenda

I'd never been to a soup kitchen and didn't know where to look for one. I decided that if anyone knew where I'd find a local soup kitchen, it would be the Bolton police department. Careful not to call the emergency line, I talked with the dispatcher.

"Do you know if there's a soup kitchen in Bolton?"

"No, I don't think there is one in Bolton, but there might be one in Clinton."

"Great!"

"Here's the number," the dispatcher said.

I thanked the dispatcher and called the Clinton police department. "Is there a soup kitchen in Clinton?"

"Sure, it's right across the street from us."

"Do you think they could use some homemade cookies?"

The officer chuckled. "Cookies? Who could turn down homemade cookies?"

"Would they take them today?"

"Well, they start serving at five o'clock every night."

I glanced at my watch. It read four-forty. *I have just enough time to drive over there.* The officer gave me directions to the soup kitchen and what door of the church to enter. I thanked him and hung up. Quickly I packed the freezer bags of cookies into big shopping bags and loaded them into the car.

From the doorway to the kitchen, I called to my husband. "Honey, I'm going to the soup kitchen. Do you want to come with me?"

"You're going where?"

"I'm taking the cookies to the soup kitchen. Do you want to come with me?"

"No, honey, that's OK."

"I'll be right back." I climbed into the car and made the five-minute drive to Clinton. Pulling into the empty parking lot, I saw that the church stood dark and quiet. Loaded with shopping bags of cookies, I entered the building. I thought it odd that it was so quiet fifteen minutes before someone would be serving a meal for many hungry people. I made my way down the hallway to where the kitchen was supposed to be. Pausing in the doorway of the kitchen, I saw light coming through the windows, lighting up the empty room. Suddenly a stranger popped up right in front of me. She startled me so badly I almost dropped the cookies.

The woman was wringing her hands in distress. "Are you my help?" she asked.

"Well . . ." I surveyed the counters stacked with grocery bags of un-prepared food and a cold range. I also saw the extreme stress registered on her face. "What seems to be the matter? What do you need?"

"You aren't going to believe this, but I've never done this before. I just came to observe—just observe! And—and—and the people who were supposed to be in charge said they had some kind of emergency. They brought all the food and left it here. I don't know what to do!"

I didn't know what to say.

"Did you see them on the way out?" she asked. "They just left. They said I would have to do this! And the people—they're going to be here in fifteen minutes. I don't know what to do!" She threw her hands into the air. "I just don't know what to do! I can do anything if you just tell me what to do. Are you my help?"

I placed my bags of cookies on the floor and took off my coat. "Of course I'll help you. We can do this. First let's get the lights on." The lights illuminated a recreation room with the chairs stacked atop the tables. "Why don't you arrange the chairs and tables while I see what food needs to be prepared."

Now if you've ever been in another person's kitchen you know that it is difficult to find your way around it. Nothing is ever where you think it might be. The miracle came when I started preparing the food. Every drawer and every cupboard that I opened held exactly what I was looking for. It seemed as though it was my kitchen. I quickly put the soup kettles on the stove to reheat the stew, put the salad in the serving trays, and took the sandwiches and placed them on a platter. Next, I assembled all the condiments and then tackled the fruit salad and the punch. With seconds to spare I raced to put the last tray on the buffet. In fifteen minutes, not with my doing but with God's, when the doors opened and the people streamed in, the food was ready to eat. There must have been about a hundred hungry people!

When I had first arrived at the church and the woman was explaining to me about the food, she had asked, "Do you know what the worst thing is?"

I shook my head. "What's the worst thing?"

"They forgot the dessert!"

My face brightened. "I've got cookies!"

She looked at me over the rim of her glasses. "But do you have enough?"

"Oh-ho-ho-ho, yes, I've got enough cookies!"

And did I ever! I placed a mound of cookies on that buffet table like they had never seen! I made sure that there was always a varied assortment and I kept filling the platter before it could be emptied completely. The people went crazy over them!

Later, as the last person went through the serving line, I glanced around the crowded room and noticed a man stuffing cookies in the pockets of his multiple layers of clothing. Grabbing a couple of handfuls of cookies, I rushed over to him. Thinking I was going to object to his stealing cookies, he tried to give some back.

"No, no! I want to give you more!" I said.

"You do?" He seemed stunned.

When some of the others saw me handing out extra cookies, they gathered around me. They wanted more too. When I placed the cookies in their hands, you would have thought I was giving them gold. I filled a lady's pocketbook with cookies. Others did like the first man, stuffing their jacket, coats, and sweater pockets. One man took off his hat. I filled it, and he carried it out like a satchel.

When the people left with the last of the cookies, they also left with big smiles on their faces. But the story doesn't end there. The lady and I washed the dishes and put them back in the cupboards, after which we looked around at the now serene and clean kitchen. My cooking partner turned to me. "You know, you're going to think I'm crazy, but I'm a Christian."

I laughed. "I don't think you're crazy. I'm a Christian too."

"You are?"

I nodded. "I'm a Seventh-day Adventist."

Her mouth dropped open in surprise. "I'm a Seventh-day Adventist, too! You know, each night of the week a church of a different denomination takes charge of serving in the soup kitchen. Saturday night is my church's turn. God not only sent me help but sent me Adventist help!"

An overwhelming flood of emotions came over us. We knelt on the hard tile floor, held hands, and thanked God for the beautiful way He answered our prayers. I could feel God's presence there with us.

This woman had no idea that my prayer for greater service had been answered in such a special way. She probably had her own reason for being there, but we thanked God together for using us. We said Goodbye without ever catching one another's name. During the meal we were too busy serving the food to exchange pleasantries. Afterward the moment was too spiritual to discuss the trivial. To this day I don't know who she was or where she came from. I don't even know if God sent an angel as part of His miracle that day. I can't even remember her face.

When I climbed into my car, I placed my shaking hands on the steering wheel and looked up into the gray, overcast New England sky. With tears streaming down my face, I prayed, "Dear God, thank You so much for using me, for showing me that You could use me. Two weeks ago when I prayed that prayer, You knew You'd need those cookies for tonight. And now You have made it abundantly clear to me that You love me and that I can be used by You. That means so much to me, dear Jesus."

From that lesson, I learned that God does have a plan for my life and that nothing happens by coincidence or chance. After I prayed that first prayer, God knew that two weeks down the road those people would forget their planned dessert—and He chose me to meet that need! I felt honored—and blessed. He could have answered my prayer the first day I prayed. Instead He taught me the lesson that everything comes in His good time, not mine.

I learned that God loves me so much that He doesn't think I'm being selfish for wanting additional blessings in serving Him. And I learned not to take the Lord for granted. He hears me. I know He answers my prayers, even the littlest, bitty prayer.

When I prayed, "If this isn't being too selfish," He knew that somewhere deep inside of me I needed to hear and see and feel His love for me. God worked a beautiful miracle in my life, and nothing was quite the same again.

This miracle changed me forever. It brought me closer to my heavenly Father than I had ever been. There was now a deep commitment to do whatever God wanted me to do, not just what I wanted God to do for me! It was probably the single most important moment in my life because I finally submitted to total dependence on God!

For the first time in my life I began to realize how selfish my previous prayers had been. I was always telling the Lord what I needed, asking Him to get me out of messes I had created for myself, asking for protection, asking for blessings for my family, always asking! It's not that this is wrong, because we do need to be able to come to our heavenly Father with our requests, but God wanted to take me a step further in His relationship with me. He knew that when I would start really living for others, I would really start living for Him. If we pray earnestly for God to lead in our lives, He surely will! I have found that the promise in Psalm 32:8 is true, "I will instruct thee and teach thee in the way which thou shalt go: I will guide thee with mine eye."

* * *

Part of my life as a preacher's kid had involved moving from one home to another and from one state to the next. Wisconsin, Michigan, Texas, and Illinois we'd at one time or another called home. Southern Illinois is where I met the Sheltons. When I was just a toddler, our family were members of the West Frankfort church, which was the Shelton family's home church. When I say the Shelton family's home church, I mean it. A lot of Sheltons attended that church. Danny's uncle Olen and aunt Mildred had thirteen children in their family alone. Danny Shelton's mother was my Cradle Roll teacher.

I loved hearing Danny and other members of his family harmonize together. Danny would play the guitar, and Tommy, his brother, the piano. I used to daydream that one day I would be able to play the piano just like Tommy. And while I do play the piano by ear, I've never made it into his league.

My sister Linda and I attended Wisconsin Academy with Danny. Two memories I have of Danny in academy are his laughter and his gift of gab. He could really talk, especially when it came to witnessing for Jesus. His enthusiasm spilled out onto everyone, as did his infectious laugh. He had a laugh that would make you laugh regardless of your mood.

Who would have imagined that Danny Shelton, the little boy my sisters and I played hide-and-seek with in our backyard on Saturday nights, would one day dream such a big dream as starting a satellite television network like 3ABN? When he launched the Three Angels Broadcasting Network in southern Illinois, Danny invited my father to preach on a

The Micheff Sisters sing regularly with Tommy Shelton on 3ABN television.

program called *Walking With the Master.* As we remembered my father calling television "devil-vision," now the irony of my father regularly appearing on the small screen brought chuckles to our lips. As a portion of the program's format, Dad arranged for my sisters and me to sing on each of his programs. Sometimes my mother would join us.

During one of our trips south to tape songs at 3ABN, my sisters and I were asked to teach some vegetarian cooking classes. Being raised vegetarian, for my sisters and me it was second nature. Mom had taught us girls to cook and bake healthy meals when we were just young children. Thus began our volunteer "career" of being 3ABN cooks. Once again God moved me further and further out of my comfort zone and into a broader service for Him.

In 1999 my sisters and I had just finished taping a cooking program at 3ABN when the vice president of the network asked if she could speak with me. Nothing could have prepared me for what she said next. "The Lord has really impressed me to ask you to do something for Him. We would like you to be the producer of a children's program called *Kids Time.*"

What? Did I hear that right? Me, a TV producer?

I was so shocked that at first I thought, *This must be a joke.* In my wildest imagination I would never have thought of producing a television show, especially one for kids. I started to rationalize all the reasons that I just wouldn't be right for the job. I proceeded down the list, stating all the barriers. I was a nurse, not a producer. I didn't know the first thing about cameras, sets, or scripts. I was used to being in front of the camera but never behind the camera. And besides, I lived near Boston, and 3ABN was in southern Illinois. But as I started to process my excuses, the Holy Spirit spoke to me.

That night I poured out my heart to God. "Lord, I've asked You so many times to show me Your plan for my life. And each time I've let You lead, it's

Linda Johnson, Tommy Shelton, Cinda Sanner, Danny Shelton, and Brenda Walsh on the set of the Micheff Sisters cooking show on 3ABN television.

been successful. Every time I take control, I have failed! Is producing this program really Your will for me? I know what it's like to run ahead of You. I've learned that lesson, and I don't ever want to relearn it."

On my knees, beside my bed, I committed my life to Him once again. I told Him I would do whatever He wanted me to do. "But, Lord, I really need to know that this is Your will!"

Thinking of the Old Testament story of Gideon asking God for a sign before leading God's troops into battle, I prayed, "Lord, on this one, I need a fleece. If You want me to produce this program, then please flood my mind with so many ideas that I'll not have a shadow of a doubt that this is indeed Your plan. And if this is not Your will, then leave me as clueless about what to do as I am right now." I arose from my knees and climbed into bed, expecting a good night's sleep.

As I flew home the next morning, my mind was already bursting with ideas. While on the plane I wrote down first one and then another. That night I could hardly sleep because my mind was racing so much. The next morning was no different. I'd barely eaten my first mouthful of cereal when the ideas started pouring in. I could do this! I could do that! Wouldn't so-and-so be perfect to do this? I wrote each fresh idea on a Post-it note. Soon there were Post-it notes all over my house. By the end of the day I had enough ideas for forty programs. "Lord, when You open the flood gates, it really pours out!"

I had so many ideas for the program that I had to narrow them down. The only element that I kept from the earlier, original show was the name, *Kids Time*. I decided to play off the word *time*. The segments became Nature Time, Music Time, Cooking Time, Praise Time, Story Time, and Sharing Time. Next I needed the on-screen talent to do each of the segments.

For the cooking segment, I wanted children to do the cooking—

Linda on the set of Story Time, with Danny Shelton's grandson, Jessie.

my nieces, Catie Sanner and Jody Micheff. Both girls knew their way around the kitchen and had the personalities to deal with the camera.

I thought my sister Linda would be perfect for Story Time. She is not only multitalented in writing, she also

Cinda on the set of a Bible story taping with Lee Jamieson, both in character.

knows her Bible backward and forward, and most important of all, she loves Jesus. Many children growing up have not heard the precious stories of Jesus. I wanted to make His life real to them.

When it came to costumes, my sister Cinda was the obvious choice. She is famous for her "theme parties." Once she had a women's ministry group over to her house for a party dressed like old-time southern belles, complete with bustles and hoop skirts. She threw theme parties based on African safaris, Hawaiian luaus, and the fifties with poodle skirts, to name just a few. Cinda went right to work on designs for *Kids Time* costumes, and my friend Virginia Gustin agreed to sew them. Virginia had been a home economics teacher and was a professional seamstress. God was leading each step of the way.

For Praise Time I needed musically gifted children. I started networking and had everyone looking for talented children who could be on the program. For Nature Time I thought of one of my father's friends, "Mr. Nature," Jim Snelling. He was not only knowledgeable about nature but had an awesome personality with just the right sense of humor to make him absolutely perfect for the job. I learned that he had moved, and I didn't know his new address or phone number.

That night when I climbed into bed and closed my eyes, I couldn't close my mind to the barrage of creativity. More ideas poured forth throughout the next day and into the third night. Finally, about two in the morning, I was desperate for sleep. "Please, Lord, could You shut off my mind for a while? I am so tired. I need some sleep!"

Then it hit me. "Oh, dear God, You answered my prayer. You have flooded me with so many ideas that it's obvious You want me to do this. You answered my prayer! As long as you want me to produce this program, I will do it—as long as You continue to hold me in Your hand." I claimed the promise in Philippians 4:13: "I can do all things through Christ who strengthens me" (NKJV).

I tried to think of reasons why I shouldn't produce the program. Tim thought it was an incredible idea, even though it meant a lot of traveling back and forth to 3ABN—after all, Bolton, Massachusetts, wasn't exactly next door to West Frankfort, Illinois. Tim always saw such great potential in me and encouraged me to do whatever I felt God was calling me to do. Our girls were older now and beginning to establish their own lives. Even though I was juggling three jobs at the time and didn't have any idea how much time the *Kids Time* "volunteer" position would take, I was ready for a new challenge—if that's what God wanted me to do.

Yes, I would do it.

With that decision made—that I would step out of my comfort zone and serve Jesus by producing children's programming at 3ABN—God was creating for me a new identity. I didn't know it at the time, but when I decided, "I'm going to produce *Kids Time*," God was in the process of giving me a new title—the title of "Miss Brenda." I have been blessed with a wonderful family, a loving husband, two delightful children, and a precious grandchild. I have enjoyed challenging jobs and being able to use my creative talents, but nothing I have ever done has equaled the joy of serving Jesus as Miss Brenda on the *Kids Time* television program. I have been truly blessed!

My first question to 3ABN about my new responsibility as producer of *Kids Time* was, "What's my budget?" I had so many creative ideas for changing the set, but I knew they would cost some money.

"Budget?" I was told. "Well, this is a kind of 'step of faith' project. There isn't a budget. There is no money for salaries, precious little for supplies, and you'll have to use the old *Kids Time* set. Maybe, after a couple of years, when money comes in, we can afford to change it."

Momentarily deflated, I went back to God. After all, if He'd given me ideas for the new set, He must also have the necessary funds tucked somewhere in His back pocket. But maybe the answer to my prayer was to wait. So I prayed again. And again He impressed me with detailed plans for a new set. I went back three times with my request to change the set. Finally I was given some hope.

"There isn't any money for a complete set change, but we can paint and put in a new carpet. That's all we can do right now."

That was wonderful news to me! I went back to my knees. "OK, Lord, You're in charge of this project. If You want me to change anything else, You'll have to open the doors."

That night I couldn't sleep for thinking about the set. At two o'clock I sat bolt upright in bed and shook Tim awake.

"Honey! She didn't say what kind of paint! She didn't say what kind of paint!"

Thinking I was experiencing some kind of nightmare, he told me to go back to sleep. But sleep was the furthest thing from my mind. Sitting up, I thought, *I'm an artist! I've been painting with oil paints for more than twenty-five years! My walls are decorated with my paintings. Maybe God gave me this talent for just this purpose—to paint the 3ABN set!* I lay back down and closed my eyes. Visions of what the set should look like paraded through my mind. There would be a Bible Time set on one side and a nature set on the other, representing God's two books—Bible and nature. And for the carpet, I'd use inexpensive green turf.

I called 3ABN the next day to schedule a time to paint the set. My faith was put to the test. "I think I'll need about two weeks."

"Two weeks? That's impossible, Brenda. The *Kids Time* set is the largest set at 3ABN. We store it in the studio. If the studio is shut down to paint, then all TV production would need to be stopped, and of course, our need for programming is so great, we couldn't afford to do that."

"I understand, of course. But there must be a way. . . ."

The voice on the other end of the phone wouldn't budge. "Two weeks is totally out of the question." We negotiated for a while. Finally I was given three days to paint the set. By the time I hung up the phone a plan formulated in my mind. I would fly in early. That way I could paint on Sunday, which would give me four days. Even with four days, the task would be humongous. But I took what I could get and scheduled the time.

I bought paints, brushes, and all the supplies I thought I would need and flew to 3ABN. After a good night's sleep, I headed over to the studio to begin this unbelievable painting project. The entire set has a total of seven panels. Each panel is ten feet high and twelve feet wide. I began by rolling sky-blue paint over the entire set. I am short, and the walls are tall. Before long my arms ached from holding the roller above my head. They shook from exhaustion. I began to wonder if I'd indeed taken on more than I could handle. Just when I thought I'd have to stop for a while, I heard a voice from the top of the stairs. It was Ben Burkhamer, who worked in master control.

"Need some help?"

"Wow! Do I ever! I never turn down good help! Can you at least get the top part for me?"

He bounded down the stairs and took the roller from my hands. With one stroke, he easily painted the top of the first panel. Every few minutes he would put down the roller, run back to the control room in time to cue up the next program to go on the air, and then run back down and continue rolling on the paint.

Half way through applying the second coat of paint, I stepped back to see if the original paint was showing through. That's when I first realized what an enormous task I'd undertaken. Overwhelmed, I concluded that it was impossible to paint the set in three weeks, let alone three days.

"O Lord, I can't do this thing You've asked of me—not alone. Please send me more help—another artist. Surely there's an artist nearby, perhaps just down the road?" I asked Him to send His Holy Spirit to impress someone to help me.

Anyone who has visited the 3ABN studios knows that its location gives new meaning to the phrase "out of the way." To pray for an artist who just happened to be living in or driving through West Frankfort, Illinois, was a big stretch, it seemed.

I'd barely prayed when a little voice in my mind said, "Call Smitty."

I ignored the Voice and continued to plead for help. I was desperate. Tears trickled down my cheeks as I wrestled with God. "Please, Lord, send another artist to help me!"

Again I heard the Voice saying, "Call Smitty."

Twenty years earlier, when we lived in California, Smitty had been my art teacher. Since the days when I knew him, Smitty had written books on art. He had traveled the world teaching art classes and sold his paintings for large sums of money. He's listed in *Who's Who in America*. I knew he'd be too busy for such a little job. And he lived in California. I needed someone in southern Illinois, and I needed them right then! So again I ignored the Voice.

Once more I cried out to God for help, and my tears flowed freely. "I can't finish this job without You! Please, please send me help!" This time I heard the Voice loud and clear.

"Call Smitty!" It was almost as if God were saying, "Brenda, don't ask Me again if you're not going to listen!"

It was so loud and clear I turned around to see if Ben had entered the studio and was speaking to me. I was alone. Gazing up at the ceiling, I wailed, "God, are You speaking to me? If You are, I will listen." I threw down my roller, ran to get my address book, and hurried to the nearest telephone.

CHAPTER 18

Smitty, Hobby Lobby, and a Whole Lot of Prayer

The first miracle was that Smitty answered the telephone. He travels so much that it is rare to find him at home. The second miracle? If I'd called an hour later he would have been on a plane for New York. And the third miracle came when I explained to him my situation.

"Smitty, is there any way you could come and help me?"

"Sure." There was no hesitation. I couldn't believe what I'd heard.

"Smitty, did you say you'd help me?"

"Yes, that's what I said. When do you need me?"

"Now!" I screamed. "I want you now!"

He chuckled at my enthusiasm. "Well, let me check the flight schedules."

Silence followed. I couldn't believe what God was doing. If anyone could pull off a miracle of painting, it was definitely my friend Smitty.

"Brenda?" His voice came back on the line. "I can land in St. Louis tonight at ten-fifteen. Will that do?"

"Yes! Yes!" My tears of distress changed to tears of delight. I'd barely hung up the phone when my friend Theresa Boote strolled into the studio wearing old clothes, ready to help me paint. Excited, I turned toward her and shouted, "He's coming! He's coming!"

Theresa, noting the tears streaming down my face, answered, "Praise God, He's coming!"

"No, no, you don't understand. I'm not talking about Jesus' return, but Smitty. He's coming!"

"Who's Smitty?"

I broke into laughter. I couldn't believe how good God was to send someone with whom I could rejoice with the minute I needed her.

"Smitty's my art teacher from California. He's flying into St. Louis tonight to help!" When I told Theresa about Smitty and how God had answered my prayer, we knelt down right then and there to thank our heavenly Father.

I thanked Theresa for her willingness to help, but I was almost finished with rolling on the background paint. No need for her to get paint all over herself, especially when she had so much work to do on her only day off. But her willing heart touched me!

I quickly returned to the set and finished rolling the rest of the walls. I was so energized that it took no time at all. I hurried back to my apartment to change clothes for the two-hour drive to the airport. Just as I headed out the door, the phone rang. It was Ben from master control.

"I have a message from Smitty."

My heart sank. "Go ahead."

"He said that all the flights to St. Louis were canceled for the evening."

My heart sank further. I could feel a new bout of tears brimming in my eyes.

Ben continued. "He says the fastest way he can get here is to fly from San Francisco to Chicago. He's already on the flight. He'll spend the night in Chicago and catch the first flight out in the morning. He'll land in St. Louis at 8:30 A.M."

I couldn't believe my ears. *Oh ye of little faith . . . Why did I ever doubt You, Lord?* My friend was willing to fly to the middle of the country, stay in a hotel for the night, then fly on to St. Louis. Talk about a miracle!

The next morning I picked up Smitty, and we were on the set painting by noon. Without a sketch or outline, we painted whatever came into our heads. The news of the visiting artist and the miracle that brought him to 3ABN spread throughout our little community. Employees of the TV ministry and visitors alike dropped by to see our progress and to meet my friend.

Midway through the project I asked him, "So, Smitty, how does it feel to be used by God in such a powerful way?" I knew the eighty-year-old man's position on God. He claimed to be an agnostic. Religion was something he refused to discuss with anyone. I'd been praying for and witnessing to him for years. I will never forget Smitty's response.

"Now, Brenda, you know how I feel about this God thing."

Brenda and Smitty on the Kids Time *set.*

I nodded and smiled. "Yes, Smitty, I know how you feel."

"But this is pretty hard evidence to ignore, isn't it?" His voice cracked a little.

I ran to him and gave him a hug. "Oh, yes, Smitty, this *is* pretty hard evidence to ignore!"

We worked until two in the morning. I was worried that he would work too hard, so I suggested we get some rest. I drove him to the 3ABN apartment that I'd arranged for him to use and had just gotten back into my apartment and crawled into bed when the phone rang. It was Smitty.

"Hey, kid, can you sleep?"

I haven't even tried yet! I thought. Muscles I hadn't used in years were aching. The mattress felt so-o-o good. "I wasn't sleeping yet."

"Me either! Let's get back to work."

We worked two and a half days on four hours of sleep. Only by God's power could we have completed such a project in such a short time. God knew that for two different artists, each with his or her own style, to work on the same canvas is difficult. So He didn't send me just any artist, but my teacher, the one who helped me develop my artistic style in the first place.

On Wednesday afternoon with our project almost completed, Smitty prepared to leave for the airport to fly to New York. As I said Goodbye, I hugged him. My friend looked frail and tired. He'd given me so much of himself. I asked him how I could ever thank him for what he'd done.

He gazed deeply into my eyes. "No, it is I who should thank you." He hugged me tightly and whispered in my ear, "Brenda, I believe."

As I watched him drive away I thought, *How wonderful is God's plan for each of us.* He could have answered my prayer for an artist in a thousand different ways, but He chose to answer my prayers for my friend and mentor at the same time. Two for one! *Truly there is no greater joy than doing service for Jesus and no safer place to live than in His plan.*

I returned to the studio and

Brenda's and Smitty's finished work on the Kids Time *set.*

spent the rest of the day adding details to the paintings—butterflies, flowers, and birds—details that directors later told me wouldn't be visible to the cameras. But since I had been taught that if a job is worth doing, it's worth doing well, these details mattered to me.

By the time I collapsed in bed at four in the morning, everything was done except for a few flowers that I intended to paint alongside the white picket fence. This left me three hours to sleep before driving to the airport for my flight home. One of the camera operators, a talented artist, offered to paint the rest of the flowers for me while I was gone. After leaving detailed instructions, I placed my paints and brushes in the makeup room where they could easily be located. I arranged to return in plenty of time should the flowers need touching up before our first taping.

A thousand dollars had been delegated to replace the carpet and repaint, a very small amount of money when you're talking about redoing a set as large as the one for *Kids Time*. Since one of the segments of the program would involve cooking, I needed a kitchen set. When I inquired, I was told a kitchen set would be more expensive than the regular set and there just wasn't enough money for that. "Couldn't you just set up a table and a hot plate?"

The more I prayed, the more certain I was that I wanted to give young children the desire to cook healthy meals, and I could hardly do this with a table and hot plate. I needed a kitchen set.

"Perhaps I could use the set from 3ABN's *Food for Thought* series."

"No! Absolutely not! We never use one set for two different programs. In order to stay true to the program, a set can be used only for its intended program."

All right, I thought, *back to my knees.* Again God told me I needed a kitchen set. Then the idea came, *What if I could change the look of the* Food for Thought *set so that the viewers wouldn't recognize it?* When I presented my idea to the appropriate powers, they agreed, with the proviso that nothing could be done to damage the original set.

The 3ABN carpenters constructed fake cabinets that could be attached to the front of the original cabinets without pounding one nail. I couldn't open any of the doors, but they looked good anyway. Finally I had a set. It was my job to make the fake cabinets look like real cabinets. *I'm an artist,* I thought, *I can do that.* I called 3ABN from my home in Bolton to say I'd be arriving a week prior to taping. "A week will give me plenty of time to get the job done."

I was told that an artist had already been hired to paint the cabinets because they didn't feel I would have enough time to get them done. "How much will that cost?" I wanted to know. "It's only going to cost three hundred dollars."

What? Why should I spend three hundred dollars *to pay someone to do something I could easily do?* Besides, that would leave me only seven hundred dollars to complete the rest of the entire set, including purchasing the carpet and buying silk plants and flowers to decorate with.

"I'm sorry," I said, "but I can't afford to waste even one penny. I'll paint the cabinets. Please tell the artist not to come."

I flew to southern Illinois ready to roll up my sleeves and paint the fake kitchen cabinets and, if necessary, touch up the flowers by the picket fence on the *Kids Time* set. My sister Linda was there to meet me. She'd driven down from Wisconsin to help me prepare for the first tapings. She'd agreed to be the Story Time coordinator, and the Bible stories were the first of the segments to be taped on the new set. She had taken on this challenge with a vengeance. She booked the actors, organized who was doing what story, and kept track of every detail through endless phone calls, costume measuring, last-minute script changes, and coordinating taping dates, times, and lodging accommodations.

I chatted away eagerly, telling Linda about Smitty and the set, eager to show her our masterpiece. When I walked onto the set, I found to my horror that the cabinet fronts had already been painted. Painted in the middle of each door was a different life-sized fern or flower. One of the cabinet fronts had ghostlike hands painted all over it. I knew it wasn't the artist's fault. He wasn't given any directions beyond painting a child's kitchen.

I swallowed hard, trying desperately not to cry. Just when I thought nothing could get worse one of the crew whispered in my ear, "Did you see the flowers on the fence yet?"

No! Not the Kids Time *set too! Not God's set!* I turned and stared in horror at the ugliest flowers I'd ever seen—all shapes and colors, leaves in purples and pinks, petals in browns and black. A three-year-old's refrigerator art would have been better. *How could this have happened?* I didn't understand.

This set was special. God had worked miracles here. This was the set Smitty and I had worked on for two and a half days! I could feel my insides shaking. I prayed that God would control my emotions, at least until I was somewhere private, away from the stares of the crew members. Just as I thought I could hold it in no longer I felt a touch on my shoulder and heard the gentle voice of Charlie Swanson, our floor director.

"Would you like me to pray with you?"

I couldn't speak, only nodded. My sister put her arm around me as Charlie began to pray. "Oh Lord, please be with my sister Brenda. You know the pain she's feeling in her heart right now. You know this isn't right, Lord, but please help her find the forgiveness in her heart toward the person who did this. And give her peace and comfort. Amen."

By the time he said Amen, my body had stopped shaking and peace flowed through me. Calmly I walked out of the studio with my dignity intact and without malice in my heart. My first destination was the vice president's office. When I told her what happened, she gasped in shock. "Here, let me handle this." I waited as she placed a few phone calls to get the details. When she finished she looked as if she would cry.

"Oh, Brenda, I am so sorry. The crew was worried that you wouldn't be here in time to finish and the camera operator who is an artist wasn't available. So a couple of the crew members tried their hand at it, and I'm afraid they had no talent in the art department! They were just trying to help!"

As frustrated as I was, what was done was done. I found a quiet corner and again took my problems to God. I prayed for the strength I would need and then returned to the studio, hoping to repair the damage that had been done to the set. I entered the makeup room and opened the cabinet where I stored my paints and brushes. The cupboard was empty. I asked a crew member if he'd seen where my equipment had been placed. He pointed to a closet. Thrown in an old bucket was what was left of my paints and my brushes. Dried paint caked the bristles. The lids of my paint containers were off, so even my paints had dried. Not able to refrain from crying, I stepped inside the closet and bawled. I dropped to my knees and pleaded with God to use someone else, someone stronger, for this assignment. "It's too much for me, Lord!"

But God had other plans—and more lessons for me to learn. By the time I finished my prayer and dried my eyes, He'd given me the strength to renew my commitment to do whatever He wanted me to do. Regardless of disappointments and setbacks, I knew God wanted me to move forward knowing that He would not allow anything to happen that wasn't in His plan.

I tried to wash the paint out of my brushes, but it was so hard that the tips of the brushes broke off. Every one of my brushes had been ruined. Several of the horsehair brushes cost fifty dollars each. Many had been gifts from Smitty.

My sister, who had been looking for me, found me inside the supply closet. She was quick to observe the redness of my eyes as I held the ruined brushes in my hand.

"So what are you going to do now?" she asked.

"Go to the store and buy new paint supplies."

"I know I'm not an artist, but you know that I'll help you in any way I can. I can paint a fence post. That shouldn't take much creativity."

I laughed. "You have such a giving heart, sis. Thank you so much." Together we worked until the wee hours of the morning repairing the damage that had been done to the picket fence. The task proved to be more challenging than we had at first imagined. It took four coats of paint to cover the ugly flowers. We worked for two days, whenever the studio was available. We munched on apples held in one hand as we painted with the other. We slept only four hours in those two days.

The night before we taped on the set for the first time, Linda and I inspected the set together. I couldn't have felt more lost. I didn't have a clue what I was doing. I'd asked for help, but it had taken so long to paint the flowers that by the time we had finished the crew had already clocked out for the evening.

Not knowing what to do, Linda and I began to fuss over the plants and the shrubs. I didn't know where to place each piece to get the best effect, but I plodded on, reasoning that all God demanded of me was my best. Finally we came to the point where we both had to admit that neither of us knew what needed to be done.

We would not panic. By now we both knew *Kids Time* was God's program and when our best-laid plans failed, He had another plan in mind—just to let us know who really was in charge! In fact, each artificial plant that I moved around the set reminded me that we have a miracle-working God.

Here's how we had obtained all those plants. With only $50 left in our budget after purchasing the fake grass carpet, I had no idea how I would be able to purchase enough plants to cover such a large set.

I prayed about this need and felt impressed to drive to Hobby Lobby in Carbondale. I knew this store had silk plants and trees. I ambled through the shop, admiring the wide selection. One particular tree caught my eye. I turned over the price tag—$399. Wow! Just for one tree!

Possessing a wholesale license through my floral business in Bolton, I knew if I could purchase them wholesale, it would come to only a fraction of the price. As I strolled back to the front of the store where the store manager was, I thought, *If only I had my wholesale supply store nearby. But that's impossible.*

"Excuse me, but are you the manager?" I asked a man who walked by.

"Yes, what can I do for you?"

"A lot, I hope." I told him I was the producer of a children's program at 3ABN called *Kids Time*. I shared with him how God had worked miracle after miracle in my life and had made it clear to me that He wanted me to do this. I told him about Smitty and how I'd left my business and a good salary in the Boston area in order to volunteer to produce God's program. He looked shocked.

"You mean to tell me that you're not getting one red cent for all the time you put in there?"

"That's right."

He shook his head in disbelief.

"I believe that there is no greater reward than to serve my Jesus."

Before he turned away, I spotted tears welling up in his eyes. He forced a cough or two.

"So you see, this set is extra special, and I know God has something special planned for it. I prayed this morning that God would impress upon me where I was supposed to go to purchase plants. And for some reason I was strongly impressed to come here. My biggest problem is that I have only fifty dollars to spend." I could imagine the man choking on that announcement. I couldn't have purchased even a small floral table arrangement for that in his shop. "I know that's not much, but look how Jesus stretched five loaves of bread and two fishes to feed five thousand people."

He smiled as though he knew the story.

"I was wondering if you by any chance have some plants on clearance or perhaps have a special sale going on."

He turned toward me and smiled. "Do you have any other shopping to do?"

I assured him I would love to look around his store for a while.

"Good. While you're shopping I'll see if there's any inventory that has been here a while that I need to clearance out. I'll come and find you when I'm done."

I gave him my biggest smile, grabbed a cart, and proceeded up one of the aisles. I wasn't shopping; I was praying for God to work a miracle. After about thirty minutes the manager motioned for me to follow him to the front of the store. I was flabbergasted to see two huge flatbed carts loaded with tall trees, shrubs, and bushes of every size.

"How do these look?" He motioned toward the overflowing carts.

I stared in amazement. "They look wonderful, but how much is it?"

He grinned. "Well, how does fifty dollars sound to you?"

My mind raced. Surely he didn't mean for all of them? I pointed to the nearest tree. "Which one is fifty dollars?"

"All of them!"

The very tree I'd admired earlier with the price tag of $399 was included. He gestured toward both carts. "I'm getting ready to hold a big clearance sale, and these were all the plants I had in the store, so if you want them, they're yours for fifty dollars even."

"Want them? Of course I want them." I was ecstatic. God had opened the windows of heaven and poured out more blessings than I could ever have imagined. Thanking him profusely, I raced back to 3ABN to get a truck big enough to hold all those plants. I was so excited, I couldn't get back to Carbondale fast enough. When I returned to the store, I loaded my treasures into the vehicle before he could change his mind and hurried back to the 3ABN studios. The words "with God all things are possible" popped into my mind as my sister and I carried the silk greenery onto the set. God had provided the set and the decorations.

But now what? I knew I needed help on how to set everything up for the cameras. We were scheduled to tape in the morning. The people who were to be on the program had come in from all over the country, but we weren't even close to being ready.

As we gazed about the set, Linda whispered, "Do you know what you're supposed to do next?"

"Uh-uh, I don't have a clue."

"I think we'd better pray about it."

"If any of you lack wisdom . . ." There on the set we joined hands and prayed, first Linda and then me. We asked for God's wisdom. We begged God to help us to know what to do. "Pour out Your blessing on this set like never before. This is Your program Lord, not ours. We dedicate it totally to You."

CHAPTER 19

Blocking the Shots

The empty television studio felt vast and foreboding to me. The television cameras stood abandoned by the crew, like three sentinels guarding a grave site at Arlington Cemetery. My high heels clicked on the concrete floor as I inspected the set one more time. By now it was after five-thirty in the afternoon. The 3ABN staff had headed home to their families for the night. My sister Linda and I believed we were alone in the building. Suddenly a door opened, and we heard footsteps coming down the back steps that lead into our building from the 3ABN radio studio.

"This is a beautiful set!"

I recognized the voice of Jozsef Palhegyi, a multitalented 3ABN photographer from Romania. He had trained to do lighting, cameras, translating, and just about anything that needed doing in a TV ministry. In my short time with 3ABN, I'd come to admire and respect the man very much.

"Thank you, but it's not my doing it's God's. I give Him all the glory. We're taping tomorrow."

Slowly Jozsef turned his gaze around the studio. "Who's helping you?" he asked.

I shrugged and rolled my eyes. "No one."

A frown settled on the man's brow. "What? Isn't anyone helping you block the shots?"

"Do what?" I had no idea what he was talking about.

"Block the shots! Isn't anyone helping you block the shots?"

Again I shook my head. I felt a little stupid because I had never heard the term before. I had been in front of the camera many times, singing with my sisters and hosting the cooking programs, but being behind the camera was a whole new experience. Jozsef shook his head.

"This is the most beautiful set at 3ABN. This just isn't right!" Out of the corner of his eye he looked at me and hesitated. "Would you like me to help you?"

Would I like him to help me? Was I hearing right? I quickly assured him I would be thrilled with any help he could give me. "I haven't a clue what I'm doing. I would be most grateful for your help!"

With that he sprang into action. He strode over to one of the cameras and turned it on. "Where do you want your wide shot?"

"Huh?" My jaw dropped. I had no idea what a wide shot was, or a narrow shot, or any other kind of shot.

He grinned at my dazed silence. "OK, if you are going to be a producer, you must learn." He led me to camera number two, where he helped me de-

Brenda blocks the shots on the Kids Time *set.*

cide exactly what I wanted to see on the set. Just when I thought I was getting the hang of it, he took me to the next camera. "Look into camera one and block the shot just like you did with the other one."

I obeyed.

"Now go back to camera two and check your wide shot again."

I peered into the lens. I couldn't believe it. The changes I'd made on camera one had ruined my wide shot. In frustration I threw my hands up in the air. "Great! Now what am I supposed to do?"

"Now, now . . ." Jozsef quickly came to my rescue. "You can do this." Step by step he taught me about lighting and shadows and much more. He used terminology I'd never heard before.

Next we focused the cameras on the Bible story scene, where I discovered a new problem. I had asked for three bookshelves from the original *Kids Time* set to be removed.

For some reason I don't understand, the carpenter had nailed half-inch boards over a hole left in the wall instead of recessing the boards to make the wall absolutely flat. Trying to make the best of the situation, Smitty and I had carefully painted scenes over the boards to minimize their presence on the wall. When Jozsef focused the camera on the wall however, the camera was unforgiving. I was shocked to see that the boards stood out like the proverbial sore thumb. They looked awful.

I straightened from peering into the camera lens and shot a pleading look toward Jozsef. He shook his head. By the grimace on his face I could tell he was also troubled by what he saw. If he felt troubled, I was panicked!

"What are we going to do? We can't leave it like that!" My blood pressure soared to dangerous new heights.

He thought for a moment before answering me. "Brenda, if I were able to recess those boards for you, would you be able to fix the painting on the wall?"

"What do you mean?"

"It's like this." As he explained our dilemma, a light went on in my brain. If I were to paint over the spot where the boards would be recessed, I would have to match the colors perfectly or the camera would reveal the difference in colors. I felt as though I couldn't breathe.

He pursed his lips and examined our problem again. "If I tore off the old boards, do you think you could blend and make the paint match?"

"Sure." I took a deep breath. At this point I was willing to do whatever it took. "Go ahead. I'm claiming Philippians 4:13, 'I can do all things through Christ who strengthens me!'"

Jozsef worked until three in the morning recessing the boards properly. He filled the cracks with wood putty until the surface was perfectly smooth. I came along behind him, carefully repainting the scenes. Where there were mountains I had to mix just the right shades of color. Where there was grass, rocks, or trees, each had to match perfectly. I knew any imperfection would show up on camera. My sister Linda stayed by and helped me during our late night repair session, even though I urged her to go back to her room and get some sleep.

"I'll go to bed when you do," Linda said. "In the meantime, I might not be able to paint your scenery, but I can be your prayer partner."

We painted and prayed until the wee hours of the morning. When we had finished and checked the results through the lens of the camera, there was no trace of an outline of the board. As tired as I was, I shouted for joy. I knew we'd accomplished our goal through God's power, not ours.

I went back to my room, took a shower, and collapsed on my bed. After getting only one hour

Jozsef Palhegyi, right, was Brenda's mentor as Kids Time *began. With Jozsef is Jim Micheff, Brenda's brother, dressed as a Bible character.*

of sleep, I woke up and prepared to go to the studio for the day's work. Before leaving my room, I called the vice president. I wanted her to know how God had used Jozsef to save the program from disaster.

"I can't tell you how much I appreciate him. He's is such a kind Christian man."

"Yes, he is."

I continued. "While I know that I have so much more to learn, Jozsef has taught me so much. Could I please have him as my mentor for at least my first week?" I knew I was pushing it to ask for him, but I had to at least try.

"Well, I'm not sure about that." She paused for a moment and then said, "Jozsef is facing a crucial deadline translating programs for another show. But I think this is important enough to pull him off that project."

Suddenly I felt weak with relief. "Thank you, thank you, thank you!" As exhausted as I felt, I knew I could face whatever adventure the day held.

It was an amazing week on the set. Jozsef was patient and kind. Any time I messed up and someone asked, "Jozsef, can you fix it?" he would say no and direct them to me. This simple act reminded the staff and me that I was indeed the show's producer, regardless of my inexperience.

Not wanting to miss anything, I followed Jozsef around like a shadow. Several times he backed up and accidentally stepped on my toes. I was amazed that every time he explained something to me, I understood it. That in itself was a miracle! I didn't have to struggle for it to make sense.

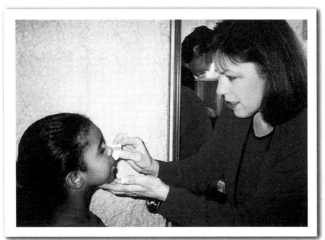

As director of Kids Time, Brenda wears many hats, including makeup

By the end of the week I felt as though I'd had a semester-long film-school course in television production. On his last day on the set, Jozsef and I sat in the control room and studied the set. I could see something wasn't right.

I pointed to the Bible story backdrop. "That village can't be in this Bible story. It doesn't make sense."

He nodded and clicked his tongue. "You're right."

"Will you go fix it for me, please?" All week long, whenever I had asked him to fix something he got up quickly and went to take care of whatever problem we were facing. This time he stayed glued to his chair. He didn't even glance my way. "No, you go fix it."

"Me?" I panicked. "Please Jozsef, do something!" He didn't budge.

Exasperated with his sudden transformation, I looked first one direction and then another. No help was coming from anyone! I ran downstairs, praying as I went that God would show me what I needed to do. I analyzed the problem from different angles, and then went to the camera operator and asked him to punch up camera three on the monitor so that I could see the scene through the lens. Then, without missing a beat, I picked up a silk tree and plopped it down in front of the offending village, being careful to set it far enough away from the wall so as not to cast a shadow and have the lighting technician upset with me.

After making certain that the tree obscured the view of the village, I ran up the stairs to the control room. The grin on Jozsef's face as I burst through the door was one I will always treasure.

"What? What's the smile for?"

He laughed out loud. "You don't need me anymore."

I feigned tears. "Oh, please don't say that. I still need you."

"No, you don't. You are a quick study, and you fixed the problem perfectly. In fact, you did something I hadn't thought of doing."

I continued to protest as he pulled himself to his feet and quietly left the room. Even though I was protesting, I did understand. God had answered my prayers. Jozsef had taught me the basics of being a producer.

Several months later I felt impressed to publicly thank Jozsef for all he had done for me. Being a very humble man, he shuns the limelight, and I knew he would try to talk me out of my little plan if I told him what I had in mind.

Unfortunately Jozsef wandered into the edit bay where Henry Juarez, our *Kids Time* editor, was typing the credits. Henry told me that Jozsef's smile turned to dismay when he read the ending of the show's credit. "A special thanks to Jozsef Palhegyi." Immediately he insisted that Henry take it off the screen.

Henry grinned and shrugged. "Sorry, I can't do that without the producer's permission."

"Well, call her immediately!"

Henry called me and put Jozsef on the line. Jozsef thanked me for thinking of him. He assured me that a special thank you was not necessary and that I should take his name off the credits.

Even as he protested I felt a sudden rush of emotion for all that Jozsef had done to make *Kids Time* a reality. It could not have succeeded without his unselfish labor of love. "Jozsef," I said, "you cannot imagine how grateful I am to you for all the help you gave me. But, no, I will not take your name off the credits. As long as I'm producing the program, your name will be a constant reminder that this is God's program and that He lovingly met our every need."

CHAPTER 20

Rounding Out the Cast

When I took on the project of producing a television program with several segments, I had no idea how complicated it would be. I quickly learned this wouldn't be Brenda Walsh's accomplishment. No one person can make a television program a success. Each segment of the program needs its own cast, its own set, and its own props. It's like producing several little programs at the same time. And everyone would need to volunteer their time!

For the Nature Time segment I knew in my heart that it had to be Jim Snelling. He and my father had joined the Seventh-day Adventist Church around the same time. When I was very young, our family had spent many delightful Saturday nights together with Jim and his wife, Jo Anne, popping corn and playing table games. My parents have remained close friends with Jim and Jo Anne throughout the years.

Through the help of a friend and a little detective work I managed to locate Jim's address and phone number. He'd retired and moved to Florida. His immediate response when I asked him to host Nature Time was, "No way! Girl, I'm retired. I've got some serious bass fishing to do!"

I was crushed. But when he laughed, I realized he was joking with me.

"Jim, you can't take this lightly," I said. "I believe the Lord has been preparing you for this job your whole life. He's handing you a worldwide ministry here."

That he didn't respond immediately was a good sign. I knew he was considering what I'd said, so I continued. "I don't want an answer right now. I want you to pray about it. But you can't take long because we're taping soon. I'll give you a call in one week. How will that do?"

The minute I hung up the phone, I began to pray. I knew it was a hard sell. Jim had a beautiful place in Florida right on a canal where he kept his boat. And he did love to fish.

Taping a Nature Time segment with Ranger Jim.

"Lord, if it is Your will that Jim take on this job, please give him no rest or peace until He makes the decision to serve You."

For two days I continued to pray. On the third day the phone rang. It was Jim. "Have you been praying for me, girl?" were the first words out of his mouth.

"You know I have."

He chuckled a little. "Well, thanks to your prayers, I haven't been able to sleep for two nights. So I'm calling to tell you that if you still want me to do it, I'm your man."

Praise the Lord for answered prayers! I felt like doing a jig right there in my kitchen. I told him that I wanted the kids to call him Ranger Jim, and that I envisioned him wearing a khaki ranger outfit, complete with a pith helmet.

"Ranger Jim? But everywhere I go the children call me Uncle Jim." He paused for a moment and then laughed. "Hey, Ranger Jim is fine. I'll do it as long as I don't have to wear women's clothing!" We laughed.

And so the character of Ranger Jim was born. Through the years since the program first aired, children have called him Ranger Jim wherever he goes. "I think you've branded me for life!" he told me. "Brenda, it is a privilege to serve Jesus in this way, and I take this responsibility very seriously. I am so thankful that you allowed me time to listen to and follow God's voice."

Two months before the taping of Music Time, I still hadn't found a host for that segment. My first choice was my good friend Marie Macri. We'd had fun working together in the junior Sabbath School department in Leominster, Massachusetts. She played the piano beautifully and had an incredible amount of enthusiasm and energy. However, when I asked her, she said, "I would love to, but my schedule will never permit it."

I wasn't surprised at her answer because I knew how busy she was. "Can you ask around and help me find someone who could do it? I'll need a group of child singers too."

Marie promised she would try to help. Hanging up the phone, I went back to my knees. "Lord, I need to find someone soon! Whoever is going to do this needs time to practice. The children who'll do this will need time to learn their songs!" But of course I didn't need to tell God that!

Next I called my mother. I knew she was planning to attend the Michigan camp meeting that weekend. I asked if she'd visit the children's departments and make a list of potential musicians for me. She agreed, although my father jokingly said he didn't know how he'd survive without Mom by his side in the adult meetings. We laughed, and I asked him to be a prayer warrior. "I need you to pray that God will lead Mom to just the right person."

Throughout the next day, which was Sabbath, I prayed for Mom as she conducted her search. In the evening the call came that I'd been waiting for. She had returned from camp meeting and was bubbling over with news from old friends she'd met. I could barely get a word in edgewise.

"But, Mom, did you get a list of names for me?"

"Well, I did the best I could. I asked everyone, but I have only five names, and I don't know anything about any of them except that they love working with children."

Five names? That was good enough for me. I wrote down the names and phone numbers. After thanking Mom for the leads I hung up and stared at the list. I didn't recognize even one name, but I knew Someone who did. Dropping to my knees, I prayed, "Lord, please lead me to the right person, the one who will best glorify You in this project. This is Your program. As always, I'm seeking Your guidance. And, Lord, when I get up from my knees, please impress upon me the name of the individual that You want in charge of Music Time. Let the very first person I call be Your choice. In Jesus' name, amen."

My hand trembled as I arose, and I sensed I was on the brink of another miracle. As many as I'd experienced since I had begun this journey, the prospect of another miracle never got old. Slowly I read the first name. *No, that's not the one.* I read the second name. *No . . .* I read the third name—Buddy Houghtaling. I read the name a second time and then a third. I didn't have any idea how to pronounce the man's last name. "Lord, this is the one, isn't it? Yes! Lord, this is the one!"

I dialed the number on the paper. A man answered. "Is Buddy there?" I didn't try to say his last name. I didn't want to get it wrong.

"Yes, this is Buddy."

"I'm Brenda Walsh, and I am the producer for a new children's program for 3ABN." He listened respectfully as I described the music segment of the show and asked if he'd be willing to host it. I knew nothing about him, had never seen him, and until that day had never heard his name, let alone his music. But I knew that I had nothing to fear if this man was God's choice for the program.

"Well," he spoke slowly and distinctly, "this sounds like a wonderful opportunity and I'd love to help you out . . ."

I thought, *Oh no, here comes the but . . .* and I was right.

"But I'm so busy. I have three kids of my own, and I have a busy dental practice. To be honest, I am swamped right now." He paused. I waited for him to continue. "Maybe it would be possible to do if we could tape the show up here in Michigan, since all the kids would be from here and . . ."

I groaned inwardly. I knew the extra cost that an on-location taping would entail, not to mention the expense of another set. "No, I'm afraid the program would have to be taped at the *Kids Time* studio here at 3ABN." I sensed he was on the verge of saying no. "Buddy, please don't give me your answer right now. I want you to pray about it. If this is God's will for your life, you surely won't want to say no. All I'm asking is that you take one week to pray about it and then give me your answer."

He took a deep breath. "All right. That sounds reasonable. And Brenda, I'll do some checking with some of the moms at church this Sabbath to recruit kids and see how many might be interested."

"Sounds good. I'll call you in a week."

The next Sunday he called me. "I'm sorry, Brenda, but I can't get any interest from any of the parents at church. I just don't see it happening."

I told him to keep praying, that his week wasn't up until midnight.

He laughed. "You don't give up easily, do you?"

"Not when the Holy Spirit is moving me!"

Two hours later the phone rang again. It was Buddy.

"Brenda? You're not going to believe this, but I felt impressed to call some members of my family, and they're all excited about the show. My sister, Robin Barrett; my nephew's wife, Arlene Leavitt; and her sister, Janean Mason, have agreed to organize it all. They also have a friend, Kathy Roderick, who has two kids, and they'll work together to make sure the children learn their songs. They'll take charge of the props and anything else that's needed, as long as I'll pick the music and host it." He'd barely paused long enough to breathe. I knew the feeling. He was as hyped as I had been the night I first considered doing the show.

"Between all of their children and my three kids, we have a group large enough to make this happen! So I guess, what I am saying is, yes, we'll do it!"

"Praise the Lord!" I shivered with excitement. Buddy and I talked a while longer about my vision for the segment. We swapped creative ideas for the program.

"Brenda, I do want to ask you for one thing. Since time is a factor here, I would like you to give the kids and me a month to practice. And then, I would like for you to fly to Michigan to hear us sing. I don't want to get to 3ABN in two months only to discover that what we practiced wasn't what you have in mind."

I didn't hesitate. "I can do that."

At the end of four weeks I flew to Michigan. My mother picked me up at the airport, and we drove to the Leavitts' home in Cedar Lake, where all the children had gathered. I sensed the kids' nervousness as I sat down to listen to them sing. As they began singing, tears of relief sprang into my eyes. Before they had finished their first song I knew beyond a doubt why God had chosen Buddy. The children's faces beamed with smiles and enthusiasm. They knew every word to their songs, and to top it all off, Buddy was amazingly gifted, not only on the keyboard but also with his incredible singing voice.

When they finished singing their song they looked eagerly at me for approval. I couldn't contain my excitement. My eyes brimmed with tears as I applauded their efforts. I could hardly speak. "I am so thrilled. You are exactly what I envisioned for Music Time!"

"Really? Do you want to hear another song?" they asked.

"Yes! Yes!" While they discussed which song to sing next, I whispered to Kathy Roderick. "Buddy is so talented! He's good enough to be a professional."

She leaned toward me. "Are you telling me that you asked Buddy to host your program and you had no idea that he has recorded professional CDs?"

My mouth dropped open. "He has a CD out?"

She nodded. "He has many CDs. He writes almost all his songs. He travels all over the country giving concerts. Plus he's on 3ABN all the time."

"What? You've got to be kidding!" I had never before heard of him, much less had a clue to his incredible talents. I was amazed at the way God had directed me to someone so talented, who possessed an energetic, downright charming personality and a wonderful sense of humor. I felt very blessed!

After the children finished their songs, they left the room for refreshments. Buddy turned to me. "What are you doing about a theme song?"

"Funny you should ask, because that is something I am currently praying about. We have tapes at 3ABN I could choose from, but that will take hours of evaluation. I've spent many hours already, and nothing jumps out at me." I knew I had to make a decision soon. The theme had to be chosen before the graphics could be designed. Jon Wood, who was working on the graphics for me, had accepted another job and would be leaving in three weeks. And there was no one, as yet, to replace him.

Cautiously Buddy asked, "Would you like for me to try and write a song for you?"

"Would I! Would you?"

He caught my enthusiasm. "Now, Brenda, I don't know if I can, but I'm willing to ask God to give me one."

"Of course, I would want it from God. I understand that you can't make a promise." We discussed what should be the criteria. "My entire focus is to first teach kids who Jesus is, and second, to share Him with others."

He thought for a moment. "We need a catchy melody that kids can hum throughout the day and that they'd recognize when they hear it and would come running to watch the program."

I agreed wholeheartedly. This was Thursday. I spent Friday and Sabbath visiting with my parents and flew home to Boston on Saturday night. I walked in the front door after 11:00 P.M. I'd barely set down my luggage when I spotted the red light blinking on the answering machine. I pressed the "Play" button.

"Hi, this is Buddy. Please call me right away when you get this message."

Oh no . . . My heart sank. *There must be a problem! Is he backing out?* I could hear the urgency in Buddy's voice. I called him back immediately. When he picked up the receiver, I apologized for calling so late.

Buddy interrupted my apology. "Brenda, it's OK. I am so excited. I think God gave me your song today!"

"Already?" Now I was excited.

"Would you like to hear it?"

"Would I?" I almost screamed.

"OK, I'm going to place the receiver on the piano so that I can play it while I sing it for you."

My pulse raced with exhilaration as I waited to hear the new song.

"It's time to share, there's a world out there, looking for a friend like Jesus . . ." Before he finished tears were rolling down my cheeks. Again I was overwhelmed by the constant flow of miracles God had provided. "Buddy! This is the theme song!"

The first day of taping the Music Time segment arrived. The set looked perfect. The camera crew stood poised in anticipation. Buddy sat at the piano, and the children stood on their mark. We'd just begun the countdown when Brad Walker, my new director, noticed that one of the cameras was out of focus. He told the cameraman to adjust the focus for a close-up on Buddy's face.

Brad checked it and then checked it again. "Brenda, what should we do about this?" He gestured toward the monitor.

I looked into the monitor. It revealed black hairs growing out of Buddy's nose.

Brad said, "Uh, Brenda, this one is your department."

Talk about a touchy situation! I ran down the stairs to the studio. "Buddy, can I see you for a moment in the makeup room?" I asked.

Thinking he needed more powder, he told the kids to stay where they were and that he would be right back. I had no idea how to deal with such a delicate problem, except head-on. Inside the makeup room, I picked up a pair of cuticle scissors.

"Buddy, I don't know how to tell you this, but on your close-up shot, we can see some hairs coming out of your nose."

Buddy burst out laughing. "Well, then snip away," he said.

I was so relieved that the man had such a great sense of humor. With the embarrassing job done, Buddy returned to the piano, and I climbed the stairs to the control room to resume the countdown.

"Five, four, three, two, one!" Buddy began to speak before singing his song. The camera moved in for a close-up. I stared into the monitor, unable to believe my eyes. Brad was doubled over with laughter.

"Cut! Cut!" He could hardly speak between his gales of laughter. By now the children and I were rolling with laughter as well. During the time it had taken Brad to give his camera operators their instructions, Buddy had snipped off some dark fur from a nearby stuffed animal and shoved it up his nose. When the camera moved in for the close-up shot an enormous piece of black fur hung from his nose. Cast and crew alike laughed until tears streamed down their faces. Buddy had relieved any tension that might have been on the set and energized the kids as well.

Buddy always drew on his sense of humor to pump up the children whenever they grew tired of retakes. If one of the children made a mistake, he would quickly take the blame for the child. "My fault, I should have done better."

Brad, the director, also considered the children's sensibilities when there was a mess-up on the set. Over the loud speaker, he would call, "Sorry, kids. I was bad, my mistake. Let's try it again." Between takes he would be found playing on the floor with the children, and they absolutely love him.

In five years of taping I never heard any of the children complain about the long hours of endless practice or all the times they had to retape a song. They never whined about missed vacations or complained about any other discomfort. Their parents have been amazing as well. They help the children learn the music long before taping. They get together as a group regularly to practice. By the time they arrive at 3ABN, they have their act together.

At the studio, each parent has his or her job to do. Some are assigned to the "smile committee"—keeping smiles on the children's faces while they sing. Kathy Roderick is assigned to the control room to cue Brad on each of the songs and what is scheduled to happen next. Others coordinate changes of outfits. Still others take care of the choreography and the props. And then, of course, some take care of preparing meals and serving snacks.

Both in the studio and filming on location, it takes a village of volunteers to make *Kids Time* successful. I am overwhelmed with the incredible talent demonstrated by caring and loving people who dedicate long hours to design sets for our *Kids Time* specials. For one Christmas special, we chose to tape in the Adventist church at Urbandale, Michigan, the church Ranger Jim attends. I asked ahead of time for them to form a decorating committee to build a set of the manger scene for the front of their church. One of the members, Todd Oftger, took on this task with great enthusi-

Buddy Houghtaling, seated at the keyboard with his wife, surrounded by the Kids Time *singers and their parents. Also pictured are the director, Brad Walker, next to Buddy at the keyboard, and the floor director, Charlie Swanson, the bearded man in the back row. Brenda is in the middle of all the kids.*

asm. When he and his volunteers finished, it was absolutely beautiful! Every detail was carefully thought of, even down to the vast canvas of dark blue sky with miniature Christmas lights twinkling as stars in the night.

At Cedar Lake, Michigan, God blessed us by performing a string of miracles through Jennie Whetstone, including, with the help of her father, Mike Noonan, providing ninety-four poinsettia plants. Jennie corralled a team of creative people to design the most amazing Bible marketplace set, which they later donated for us to use at 3ABN to tape Bible stories for Story Time. Frank and Angie Kurtz even took their vacation and not only brought the set to us but stayed all week to set it up! God is so good!

In addition to producing *Kids Time,* I am now producing *Kids Time Praise.* Producing one television program had been taking all my time. How could I possibly produce a second? God reminded me that He is in charge and all I had to do was be willing. God sent me so many musically gifted children, not to mention the incredibly gifted Mark Bond and his musically talented family. Their family had come several times to tape music for *Kids Time.* The thing I love most about them is how much they love Jesus!

Mark is also a graphics artist. When I called Mark and asked him if he would be willing to volunteer his time to create an opening graphic for *Kids Time Praise,* he responded with an immediate "Yes!" He not only created the graphics for that program but also did all the graphics for the new *Kids Time* cook book, *Cooking With Catie!* His willingness to use his talents as a graphic designer, both

Mark and Conna Bond with their children, singing on the Kids Time *set.*

with video and print, continues to amaze me. His wife, Conna, home-schools their four children yet still has time to volunteer too. She writes all my openings for *Kids Time*. For four years, Ruth Redding Brand had written my openings but, due to an increased work schedule, was unable to write them anymore. God sent Conna to pick up the load. He always has a plan. Conna says that even her children help and are blessed by it.

When I prayed earnestly that God would lead us to someone who could take charge of our costuming department, He impressed on me to call Lucy Neuharth. Previously Lucy had taped a Bible story for me, and I remembered her saying that she was a seamstress. I went to the telephone to call her, but before I picked up the phone I noticed that the light was blinking on my answering machine. It said I had one message. I heard, "Hi, this is Lucy Neuharth, remember me? I'm a seamstress and I'd love to volunteer for *Kids Time*. If you could use my help, please call me." And she left her phone number and email address.

My heart beat faster as I picked up the phone to call her back. I knew God had answered my prayer even before I asked. After a few pleasantries I told her my reason for calling. Would she make the costumes for the program? She almost started crying.

"I would be honored to sew for *Kids Time*!"

What a blessing Lucy has been. She has sewn hundreds of costumes for all ages and all sizes. They are so well done she could easily make a profitable living selling costumes in Hollywood.

When I answer the *Kids Time* mail, I send every child a *Kids Time Activity Book* along with a bookmark. Some very special people in Massachusetts, who love Jesus very much, make these book-

Lucy Neuharth has sewn hundreds of costumes for Kids Time.

marks. Margie Holden, along with her daughters, Polly, Ellie, Margie, Susie, and Sally, has a bookmark ministry. These special treasures have beautiful pictures of nature, and they also include a Bible verse. The Holdens have made literally thousands of these bookmarks for *Kids Time* over the past five years, and children all over the world are being blessed by them. I praise God for their faithfulness!

Kids Time had been on the air for two years when God impressed me that we should have Bible studies for kids. I prayed and prayed about it, and God opened the doors of heaven and

Margie Holden, right, bookmark maker for Kids Time, *with Linda Kay at her high school graduation.*

poured out His blessing. The result? *Kids Club* was born, and when kids join the club, they receive Bible studies. There are a total of fifty-two lessons, and they are mailed out six at a time. When they complete the lessons, the kids are then able to use those lessons to give Bible studies to their friends.

There were so many kids enrolled the first year that I was not able to keep up. My precious mother stepped up to help me out. She is in charge of *Kids Club* now, and I don't know what I would do without her. She keeps track of every lesson and every child, no matter what country they are from. At the time this book is published, there are well over three thousand children signed up for *Kids Club* from more than twenty countries! As my dad would say, "That's a big Praise the Lord!"

My life is consumed with *Kids Time*. When I'm not actually on the set taping, I am spending hours and hours booking the next programs, answering letters, viewing videotapes that children send to me, and recruiting!

CHAPTER 21

Overpaid

I am often asked where I find the musically gifted children who appear on the *Kids Time* television program. I tell them, "God." I pray about everything. Wherever I go, I am always networking and recruiting. I have friends and acquaintances keeping their eyes and ears open to possible talent. I love getting calls telling me about a child they heard at church or a friend's friend whose daughter plays the violin "like an angel."

The first month I was responsible for producing *Kids Time* I called so many people that my phone bill was more than nine hundred dollars. After my husband recovered from the shock, he placed me on a more reasonable telephone plan. I use an average of thirty-five hundred minutes on my cell phone each month.

My goal for the Sharing Time segment was to involve children from around the world. I wanted them to tell me how they shared Jesus with others. I wanted viewers to say, "Wow! If she or he could do that, maybe I could too!"

Brenda on the Kids Time *set with the Cadet sisters.*

In the beginning I had a problem. I had no letters. I realized that it would take time to build up a portfolio of letters from the viewers. Where could I start? Having attended so many church schools in my childhood, I decided to start there. I would visit schools and encourage the children to write to me so that I could begin taping this segment.

My first visit was to a school near my home. It was the largest Seventh-day Adventist church school in New England. The principal was delighted to have me come and present my request to their joint worship. After being announced, I stood in front of more than a hundred squirming, wriggling children between the ages of six and thirteen.

I told the children about the *Kids Time* program and about Sharing Time in particular. And then I explained what I needed from them. "All right, boys and girls, how many of you have witnessed for Jesus?"

Almost every hand flew into the air. Was I ever excited! I pointed to one little girl in the front row who was wildly waving her hand. "Can you tell me what you've done to share Jesus?"

The girl looked horrified, shook her head, stammered "No," and quickly tucked her hands close to her chest. I smiled and asked another child and another, but was met with "I don't know" from all of them. Out of a hundred children who were present, only three could tell me what they had done to share Jesus with others, and all their answers were the same. "I went to sing at a nursing home."

Now don't get me wrong. Singing in nursing homes is wonderful. But there are so many other ways to share Jesus. More than I realized when I conceived of doing this segment, there was a dire need to show children around the world that there are thousands of ways to share God's love with others.

From an early age I'd been encouraged to witness for Jesus. Whether it was singing at a hospital, or passing out literature at the grocery store, or making food for shut-ins, my parents taught me the importance of witnessing to others. I couldn't help wondering, *Is it possible that kids today aren't witnessing because their parents aren't witnessing?* I visited more than twenty schools before I had enough letters to start taping the first program. After the program aired, I never needed to ask again. Once that episode of *Kids Time* aired, the letters poured in to the studio. Praise God!

I receive letters, both postal and email, from children all over the world, sometimes as many as two hundred in a week. The letters inspire me. I can be having a most discouraging day and trudge to my office and open a letter from a child, and then I am reminded all over again why I do what I do.

For example, when I received this letter, I didn't realize at the time how far its effects would reach:

Dear Miss Brenda,

My daddy drinks and gets mad at my mom and she cries. I share Jesus by telling my dad not to drink so much. I don't like it when my mommy cries. Miss Brenda, would you please pray for my daddy too? I love you.

—Nicole

P.S. Here is my picture.

When I read Nicole's letter on the air, I held up her picture. I asked the boys and girls around the world to pray for Nicole's daddy.

Two years later, following a 3ABN rally, a little girl asked to speak to me. She had waited patiently in a long line of people to greet me. When her turn finally arrived, she said, "Miss Brenda, do you remember me?"

I sent up a quick prayer for God to bring her name to my mind. I answered, "Why, your name is Nicole. You wrote me a letter about your father!"

"Yes! Yes! That's me. See, Daddy, I told you Miss Brenda would remember me!" She pulled the man behind her closer to me.

"Daddy, this is Miss Brenda. Tell her, Daddy, tell her."

Shyly, the man told me his story. "About two years ago I was sitting in the living room reading the paper while my daughter was watching your show. I was waiting for it to end so that I could watch my program. I looked up and saw my daughter's photo on the screen. Naturally I put down my paper and listened as you read the letter Nicole had written." Tears filled his eyes. He cleared his throat. "When you asked all the boys and girls all over the world to pray for me, something happened to me that I can't begin to describe. I had to leave the room quickly so that my daughter wouldn't see my tears. Just to think that my little girl loved me so much that she would write a letter to a complete stranger to ask for prayer for me was more than I could take."

By now both of us had tears in our eyes. He continued, "You have no way of knowing this, but you also saved my marriage. My wife had decided to leave me. You changed my life forever. Not only did I quit drinking, but I was baptized last year, and now we attend church as a family. Thank you so much for what you do for the children and also for us parents." Our tears mingled as I hugged them both and silently thanked God for the privilege of serving Him this way.

Sometimes I'm not sure what to do about a letter.

Dear Miss Brenda,

I am from the beautiful island of St. Lucia in the West Indies. I do not have much food or money, and my parents are dead. I live with my grandma who does not want me. Please pray for me because I want to die. I lie awake at night thinking of ways I can kill myself, but I am too afraid. I am 11 years old. Please pray that I can die.

Love, Alicia

Sadly there was no return address, so I couldn't respond personally to her. But I prayed that God would wrap her in His arms, and give her hope and a desire to live for Him.

Many of the letters I receive are from children who are mistreated at school or abused by a parent. These hurting children reach out to the hope of Jesus that is presented on *Kids Time*. One little girl, Candice from South Africa, runs home from school each day to send me an email. She tells me about her day at school and about all the ways she's shared Jesus with others. In one letter she told me about a girl at her school that nobody liked. The other children made fun of her because she was so ugly. "She always sits by herself in the cafeteria during lunch. But today, I went to sit next to her. I told her I would be her friend. I think I shared Jesus with her. What do you think?"

My favorite letters are the ones from children who tell me they've given their hearts to Jesus and are being baptized. Last summer, I met a ten-year-old girl who came up to me after an altar call I gave and asked, "Miss Brenda, I want to give my heart to Jesus, but I don't know how."

All the long miles on the road, all the hours and hours on the phone, all the days spent away from my own family, seem so small a sacrifice for these precious little souls.

I say "little," but I've learned that God's children come in all ages and sizes. A few years back when I was still living in Massachusetts, Christmas was coming and I needed to buy gifts for my family. As it goes at Christmas time, I'd been so rushed I had left my gift buying until the last minute. It was a Friday afternoon. Frantic to get everything done, I rushed to the mall, parked my car, ran inside, and started up the escalator. As my foot touched the moving staircase, I heard a man's voice shout, "It's Brenda Walsh! It's Brenda Walsh!"

I turned to see a rough-looking man pointing at me. His dirty jeans and torn denim jacket didn't reassure me, nor did the chains hanging from his belt loops and the tattoos on his hands and neck. The scars on his face indicated he'd been in some fights or an accident. He looked as though he'd seen a ghost. He pointed again. "Look! It's Brenda Walsh! It's the cookie lady!"

By now everyone else was staring at me as if to say, "So who's Brenda Walsh?" He was waiting for me as I stepped off the escalator. His whole body shook; he could barely speak. "You're the cookie lady, right?"

I nodded yes.

Continuing to point, he repeated over and over, "It's a sign! It's a sign!"

"Sir, what is the matter?" I gently put my hand on his arm to calm him down. "You seem upset. Can you tell me what it was about the cookie story that upset you so?"

He took a deep breath. As he pushed a strand of long hair away from his face I was momentarily distracted by the collection of gold earrings piercing both ears. *There must be ten in each ear!*

"I'm not a very good person. In fact I couldn't tell you any good thing about myself. I've done a lot of bad things, things I'm not proud of. I've been in and out of prison; in fact I got out yesterday." His voice was thick with emotion. "I was at my mom's house last night. I flipped on the TV while she was in the kitchen cooking my first home-cooked meal. That's when I happened to see you on the screen and when the announcer mentioned Bolton, Massachusetts, I stopped to listen, because my mom lives close by."

He took a deep breath and swallowed hard. "Well, I watched the whole thing, and when you were done telling your cookie story, I was crying like a baby. I've never seen anything like that before—God really answering prayer and all."

I could tell he was fighting to control his emotions. "Then I kinda got mad at God. I looked up at the ceiling and, right out loud, I told God that if He was real, if there really is a God, then send me a sign like you did for Brenda Walsh. I said, 'That's right, God. I'll make a deal with You. You send me a sign, and I'll give my heart to You—like the cookie lady!' " Tears were streaming down his face. "What do you think the chances are that I'd see the cookie lady in the mall the very next day?"

By now I had tears in my eyes as well. "Sir, I believe God answered your prayer. I believe He has given you the sign you asked for, because Jesus loves you and He heard your cry. There is indeed a God!"

The man gave his heart to God right there in the mall, and I left him on a spiritual high! What an affirmation that God was still working with me and through me in a special way. Somehow the sparkly trinkets in the display cases in the stores and the sweet-smelling perfumes in the department stores lost their attraction for me. Everything else pales in comparison to souls being won for Christ!

Recently I received a call from a woman in California. She asked, "Is this Brenda Walsh from *Kids Time?*"

"Yes, this is she."

"You mean it's really you?"

"Yes."

"I can't believe it! I'm talking to Miss Brenda! You don't mind if I call you Miss Brenda, do you? That's what I hear the children call you on *Kids Time.*"

"No, that's fine. What can I do for you?"

"Well, I just had to tell you that I am a fifty-six-year-old kid, and I love *Kids Time.* I'm not an Adventist. But about two years ago I started watching your show. I just love those little kids, and are they ever talented!"

I smiled to myself at her enthusiasm.

"I have a confession to make. I'm not a kid, but I signed up for Kids Club and started taking your Bible studies. I hope I didn't take the lessons away from some other child. I was so excited to hear all the stories about Jesus. And, Miss Brenda, I found out that you are right. It always amazed me how you talked about Jesus like He is a real person. I found out He really is!"

By now her excitement had become mine.

"I'm trying to tell you that I found Jesus as my personal Savior, and I know He loves me. I even went out and bought myself a Bible. I've been going to church for thirty years, and I've never owned a Bible. I finished all the lessons, and I framed my activity book that you sent as a reminder of how I found Jesus." Her tone changed when she continued. "I went to my church and told all my friends, but my priest talked to me and told me that he doesn't want me talking so much about Jesus. Well, it's hard, you know, not to tell them when you love Him so much. I just couldn't help myself.

"I told them all about Jesus and about 3ABN. I told them that Sunday isn't Sabbath and that Saturday is the day to worship. My priest told me I could not come back to church. So you know what I'm doing? I'm attending your church. And I just love it!"

A mother in the Philippines wrote to say that she found Jesus while watching *Kids Time*. She said she'd never been a Christian and didn't know Jesus. Her husband had died and left her with four children. With work keeping her away from home so much, her children didn't have the proper training and were not as well disciplined as she'd like. In fact, they were so disobedient, she said she didn't even like them anymore. For a time she'd considered abandoning them on the street. A neighbor gave her a television, and the children found a program they loved to watch—*Kids Time*.

The children's behavior improved. They began asking their mother questions about Jesus—who He was and whether He really loved them. She decided to begin watching the show so that she could learn what they were talking about. After several months they asked if they could go to Miss Brenda's church. She found a Seventh-day Adventist church and had been attending ever since. "You have changed our lives. My children are loving and thoughtful. They love Jesus, and I do too. We all got baptized last year. I just had to say thank you." Are there enough praises in heaven and earth for testimonies like that?

One Sunday, just before I was to leave my home in Tennessee to re-turn to the 3ABN studios in southern Illinois, I was feeling sorry for myself. I hadn't had time to wash clothes or even unpack my suitcase from my previous trip. My house needed dusting; my floors needed sweeping. I had a zillion letters stacked on my desk that needed answer-ing. I did not want to climb into my car and drive for six hours. I just wanted to stay home, sleep in my own bed, cook in my own kitchen, and relax in my living room with my husband.

I glanced at the kitchen clock. It was almost noon. I would have to leave soon if I didn't want to drive in the dark. Realizing that I lacked the right spirit, I prayed, "Dear Jesus, please give me a clean heart and renew my spirit. You know I want to be selfish and just stay home. But Lord, You also know my heart, and You know that I love You, so please place a sweet spirit within me. Lord, make me willing because I am weak. Amen."

Using all the energy I could muster, I dragged myself into my bed-room and stuffed clothes into my suitcase. "Let's see, I need deodorant, panty-hose, my toothbrush . . ." The list seemed endless. Thirty minutes later as I grudgingly loaded my luggage in the trunk of the car, the phone rang.

"Hello, is this Brenda Walsh?" It was a man's voice.

"Yes."

"The Brenda Walsh from *Kids Time?*"

"Yes, this is the Brenda Walsh from *Kids Time.*"

"I can't believe it! I'm really speaking with you. I want you to know that I have been waiting two years to talk to you! I am a Seventh-day Adventist today because of *Kids Time.*"

Suddenly he had my full attention.

"I'm calling from Perth, Australia. *Kids Time* comes on about nine-thirty each evening here. My wife and I were getting ready for bed one night. And while I was waiting for her to brush her teeth I started flip-ping through the channels on the tellie. I came across the most adorable little kids—they were so talented, they sucked me right in, they did! I called to my wife to come watch too.

"To make a long story short, we both just loved *Kids Time.* We started watching it every night. We wouldn't go to bed without watching your show. But one night we turned on the tellie too late, and you were just going off the air. We were so disappointed we missed it that the next night we turned it on early."

My excitement was building as I continued to listen to the man's story.

"While we were waiting for your show to come on we became interested in the message of truth that we heard. We were baptized six months ago, and now we attend your church. I wanted to tell you earlier, but no one would give me your number. Then I happened to see your advertisement for a CD and, lo and behold, there was your phone number. I gave a quick jot down and well, here I am! Thank you for all you're doing for Jesus."

When he hung up, I dropped to my knees and thanked God for His loving mercy. "Lord, You could have had this man call me two years ago, but instead You let him call me today, right when I needed the encouragement. You always know just what I need. Thank You Jesus for affirming me today."

I packed the car in record time. The six-hour drive passed in what seemed like six minutes. I praised my Jesus all the way to Illinois. There truly is no greater joy than serving Jesus.

Whenever the evidence of one of God's precious blessing comes my way, whether it be in a letter, a phone call, or a face-to-face miracle, I call my dad to share it with him. His response to me is, "Bibby, you are overpaid!" And he's right!

Family Photos

Brenda and Tim at home.

Tim with Becky at her wedding rehearsal dinner

Tim with Linda Kay

Becky with her new husband, David Coffin, and grandparents Nana and Papa Micheff.

Brenda with her first grandson, Michael, who calls himself "Grandma's boy."

Cinda, Brenda, and Linda with Grandma Micheff

Cinda, Jim, Brenda, Kenny, and Linda on the Sabbath that Jim and Kenny were ordained to the ministry.

Back row, L to R: Jim Johnson, Linda Johnson, Jimmy Johnson, Jamie Micheff, Jim Micheff, Jr., James Micheff, Sr., Becky Walsh, Tim Walsh, Joel Sanner, Cinda Sanner, Catie Sanner, David Sanner.

Front row, L to R: Jason Micheff, Jenny Micheff, Gail Micheff, Jody Micheff (sitting on floor), Bernice Micheff, Brenda Walsh, Linda Kay Walsh, Tammy Micheff (sitting on floor), Ken Micheff, Crystal Micheff (sitting on floor), Jeremy Micheff.

Epilogue

When Jesus walked on the rough roads of this wicked world, He had a special ministry for women who were taken advantage of and shunned.

He had an intimate conversation with the Samaritan woman and asked her to serve Him, even though she had a sordid reputation when it came to men. He took special notice of the unclean woman who was rejected because of continual bleeding, and He healed her. He accepted the attentions and spontaneous acts of love and sacrifice from a woman who had sold herself to men.

And two thousand years later, *He redeemed me!* He took me from a prison of pain and opened up to me an unlimited opportunity to serve Him and be a blessing to millions through a worldwide television ministry.

I may not have the opportunity to break the alabaster box for my Savior,

I may not be able to give Him a drink of cool water, but . . .

I can praise Him and give Him the glory . . .

. . . for picking me up when my life was in shambles;

. . . for rescuing me from abuse and disgrace;

. . . for pulling me up from the pit of despair when the devil was so desperately trying to push me down;

. . . and for giving me the desires of my heart.

I will forever sing His praises, for He broke all the rules of rational reasoning to allow me to experience His miracles of grace.

At eighteen, I thought my life was over. When I was beaten and bruised, I thought it was my fault. My dreams were shattered. I had no hope.

What happened next is best summed up in Psalm 40:1–3:

I waited patiently for the LORD; he turned to me and heard my cry.
He lifted me out of the slimy pit, out of the mud and mire;
he set my feet on a rock and gave me a firm place to stand.
He put a new song in my mouth, a hymn of praise to our God.
Many will see and fear and put their trust in the LORD (NIV, italics supplied).

By choice I am a cherished daughter of the King of the universe, washed clean in the blood of Jesus Christ, and consecrated to His service. No matter how low I believed I had fallen, no matter how crushed my body and my spirit appeared to be, God healed my brokenness. He lifted me up to unbelievable heights and today allows me to fly with the eagles.

And you know what?

He will do the same for you.

Also by Brenda Walsh (and her sisters):

Cooking With the Micheff Sisters.
You've seen them on TV singing and cooking. Now 3ABN regulars Brenda, Cinda, and Linda have put their favorite recipes in a vegan vegetarian cookbook that proves that good taste and good health do go together. More than 100 recipes. Color photographs.
0-8163-1994-4. Paperback.

Other true life dramas you'll enjoy:

Abandoned but not Alone
John Lomacang. Millions have heard the former Heritage Singer minister in song. Now read the thrilling testimony of how God helped John put his family back together again after being abandoned by his mother as a child.
0-8163-1914-6. Paperback.

Set Free
Michael and Amber Harris with James Ponder. Set Free is more than a story about drug abuse, a tragic accident, and paralysis. It's an unforgettable love story about a spiritually-broken man, a physically broken woman, and an all-powerful, all-loving God who specializes in mending broken people. It is virtually impossible to read this story without being moved first to tears, and then moved to embrace and praise the God who makes us all "free indeed."
0-8163-2039-X. Paperback.

Order from your ABC by calling **1-800-765-6955**, or get online and shop our virtual store at **www.AdventistBookCenter.com**.
• Read a chapter from your favorite book
• Order online
• Sign up for email notices on new products

Prices subject to change without notice.